Coming Back to Faith

The Journey from Crisis of Belief toward Healthy Engagement

Meditative Signposts from the Christian Year

J. LeBron McBride, PhD

ISBN 978-1-64114-676-0 (paperback)
ISBN 978-1-64114-754-5 (hardcover)
ISBN 978-1-64114-677-7 (digital)

Christian Faith Publishing, Inc.
832 Park Avenue
Meadville, PA 16335
www.christianfaithpublishing.com

Printed in the United States of America

Lovingly dedicated to my wife, Deborah Walden-McBride, a family nurse practitioner. You have been my faithful companion on many walks (literally and figuratively) along the journey for some twenty-seven years. Thank you!

To my boss, Frank R. DonDiego, MD, a full-breadth family physician who approaches the whole person with compassion. You gave me the opportunity to work in medical education some twenty-five years ago, and it has enhanced my journey. Thank you!

To those who desire to find the way back from the turmoil of a crisis of belief. I hope you find in these pages broad and practical concepts for the rebuilding or renewing of your faith.

Contents

Preface...9

Introduction

  1   Finding the Way Home................................15

Epiphany/New Year

  2   Arise and Seize the New Year on a New
       Journey of Faith...29

  3   You Are Loved by God: Can You Accept
       This Fact and Start Living by it? 34

  4   In God, Find a Beacon of Orientation for
       the New Year! 39

The Lenten Season

  5   Ash Wednesday: Doing the Math
       What Do You Need to Add or Subtract
       from Your Life?..47

  6   Knowing That God Is Pleased with You
       Opens Up All Kinds of Possibilities! 51

  7   Journey into the Wilderness:
       On the Tiptoe of Expectation!.....................57

  8   What Are You Avoiding on the Journey?:
       Detours Can Be Dangerous...........................63

  9   Temptation: The Seduction of Power 67

  10   Temptation:
       Risking Too Much for the Wrong Reasons 73

The Transfiguration

11 The Mountaintop and Valley Experience on
    the Journey of Faith......................................83

Holy Week

12 Palm Sunday: The Steadfast Focus of Jesus
    During the Ups and Downs of Life 91
13 A Fragrance or a Stink—the Contrast Is Clear.............96
14 Maundy Thursday: What an Example for
    the Journey!..101
15 Good Friday: The End Is the Beginning! 105
16 Good Friday: The End Is Not the End! 108
17 Easter: Your Passion Can Live Again!......................111
18 Easter: Weeping May Linger for a Night,
    but Joy Returns! 117

Pentecost

19 The Spirit at Work 125

Post-Easter Ordinary Time

20 Stumbling and Falling but on the Road with
    Jesus Again! 135
21 We Will Not Be Ordinary Christians:
    Called to Love as Christ Loved! 141
22 When the Groans and Moans of Life Are
    Too Great to Bear...146

Fourth of July

23 Freedom and Independence for the Christian.............155

World Communion Sunday

24 How Wide Is Your Table? How Big is Your Heart?......165

All Saints' Day

    25   When Is the Last Time You Saw a Saint? 175

Thanksgiving

    26   Are You Taking the Proper Dosage of
           Thankfulness for the Journey? 183

    27   Gratitude Can Change an Attitude!............................188

The Season of Advent

    28   First Sunday of Advent: Prepare for the
           Journey toward Hope! 199

    29   Second Sunday of Advent: Journey Away
           from Chaos to Peace......................................206

    30   Third Sunday of Advent: Packing Joy into
           Your Suitcase for the Journey........................212

    31   Fourth Sunday of Advent: The Return to
           What Matters—Love.....................................217

    32   The Longest Night Service: Moving from
           Nope to Hope 222

    33   Christmas Eve: Following the Light............227

    34   Christmas: Let's Cancel Christmas ... or
           Should We? 230

The Closing of the Old Year

    35   It Is Time to Let Go of the Past and Move Forward!...239

Epilogue...247

References 249

Preface

I have a profound respect for the many sincere persons who have legitimately left the Christian faith. I am writing about those who have honestly and authentically struggled and found that their beliefs no longer hold meaning, those who have been deeply wounded in various ways by their religious institution, and those who can no longer find any practical relevance in their former faith. Some have called these persons "the church alumni,[1]" and they number in the millions.

This book is for all who desire to find a practical meaning in their faith and is especially for those who have left the faith literally or emotionally and intellectually and are attempting to find a way to return. Some have been caught in toxic religious institutions. Others have simply found that earlier beliefs do not hold the same meaning. Some have reactively rejected their past for whatever reason. Many, at some point, desire to come back to faith but realize that they can no longer find a home in their former belief system. They may never be able to return to the mode of Christianity of prior years; however, they may find that a broader and healthier approach can be an authentic pathway to come back to faith. This book is not about arguing theology or presenting minute developments of systematic beliefs. It paints, instead, broad, practical, and pastoral stokes of Christianity that can enhance life and give purpose.

The work provides an avenue to begin the journey back toward the great pastoral themes of Christianity without all the baggage that is often attached to the Christian faith by those who desire to present their own brand of the faith. Often, it is not Christianity per se that sincere people reject but a literalistic and overdeveloped performance and behavior oriented perversion of the faith. The book presents simple and practical themes for living life with a Christian orientation. I no longer believe that it is essential to argue about finer points of theology in order for a faith to be helpful and sustainable.

I also have had rebellion, anger, disillusionment, and frustration with my faith system. My faith has evolved, but I have somehow been able to stay connected to and involved in the Christian community. However, my faith is no longer as complicated as previously. It is also no longer so detailed in precise theology. I no longer have to have all the answers or even need to answer all questions of living. However, I have come to discover that the broad themes and beliefs of my faith continue to hold relevance for my daily life.

This book is an attempt to follow the great pastoral themes of Christianity that have developed into the Christian year and to find practical and helpful motivations in them. I use the Christian year with some freedom and adjustment and added the Fourth of July—the Independence Day of the USA—and Thanksgiving for those of us in the United States. I also added a meditation on the transfiguration and a meditation on closing of the year. I also begin the year with January 1 and New Year's Day, or Epiphany, rather than with the season of Advent since our calendar year begins that way.

It is the pastoral part of my belief system that has become so very relevant to me and I find resonates with the persons in my ministry and counseling as well. The broad pastoral themes of hope, purpose, passion, loyalty, humility, thankfulness, service, discipline, acceptance, grace, affirmation, identity, and so on appear to me to be free from the rigid frameworks that many have developed or imposed upon Christianity and, in my opinion, often distorted its value. These great pastoral themes give us room to move and flex our beings and personalities on our journey of life and faith as well as to live honestly and authentically with our faith. Many can come back to faith by focusing on these themes and find practical help and hope for living life in them. May this be true for you.

How to read this book: I would suggest reading the introduction if you have been reactive to your former faith or if you have been in a more toxic religious environment and are leaving that behind. If you do not want to think about organizational religious struggles and journeys then you may want to jump right in at chapter 2. I would encourage you to read only a chapter per day and to reflect upon the themes presented.

Once you have read the book through, you may want to pick it up again as the days of the Christian year come around to review and center upon those great themes. May you enjoy the journey into the themes offered by the Christian year that, on a yearly basis, call us to reach our full human and spiritual potential. My hope is that the days of the Christian year as discussed in these chapters will truly be signposts along the way toward healthy faith for you. May this book move you toward healing, happiness, and wholeness. Enjoy!

Introduction

1

Finding the Way Home

This chapter is particularly for those who have been sidetracked by their own or their religious organization's distortion or myopic focus. Legalism and institutional forms of control, power, and bias can be a toxic mix. Sometimes, it is not that religion is the problem but that we or the institutions to which we belong use belief in psychologically and theologically sick ways. This book provides help from the emotional and spiritual brink of disaster toward positive and healthy integration of broad Christian concepts.

Just as a diamond has more than one sparkle, so theological transitions have more than one dimension. Most people who come to new theological understandings do so by diligent study and reflection; they soak in their new discoveries like sponges absorbing water. Usually, people come to intellectual insights that are freeing, resonating with their new spiritual convictions. Others have been reactive and are so fed up that they just either suddenly or gradually let go of beliefs that have been a part of their lives, at times without great study or reflection.

They may have simply wandered away from any formal belief structure and are somehow lost in the wilderness of believing but not really believing or culturally living in a spiritual ghetto that is devoid of sustenance. However, in the whirlwind of the excitement of their new discoveries or, on the other hand, rejection of long-held beliefs, people often neglect a vital piece of the transition puzzle. Far too often, sincere persons are unprepared for the emotional impact of a theological awakening or theological reaction, especially when they have been intertwined in a toxic and controlling church or have been more attached to their beliefs than they realized. In fact, the emotional conflict may prove almost unbearable. People may get lost in a devastating transitional wilderness where life feels barren and desolate and the fierce monsters of loneliness, grief, anger, depression, anxiety, and many other powerful emotions show their fangs—and appear ready to devour them.

Toxic Structures and Their Psychological Walls

This chapter will address the intense emotional and psychological dimension that may accompany a transition in belief and belief identity. Oftentimes, toxic churches or even well-established religious systems have, over time, built psychological walls beyond which are wasteland moats around their closed systems. In attempting to leave the system, one has to maneuver among emotional predators to find true freedom.

For example, teachings stating that a certain church is the only true church, the remnant or last-day church are psychological barriers that can be difficult to destroy. Further, destructive churches often develop very strong myths among the members that if they leave the organization, they will be eternally cursed or damned and will not survive spiritually. When a church's theology supports a closed system and limited or no interaction with "outsiders" who worship differently or who have the "mark of the beast" or some other apocalyptic mark, many fear the wilderness that lies outside that church is too threatening to risk experiencing. Anyone who once accepted such teachings or has been brainwashed by them should not minimize the powerful addiction to the church they ensure.

These tactics make it very difficult for members to explore options intellectually and emotionally. Again, even when one does somehow break free enough to come to new intellectual and spiritual understanding, the psychological impact of abandoning those teachings may be what sneaks up and destabilizes the person. Those who do venture out of an unhealthy church or long-held belief system do best if they know of the psychological and emotional dangers ahead.

The other side of the picture is those who have become reactive and antagonistic toward old belief structures and have left them. Some, after an initial period of separation, find themselves longing for more structure in their belief system. They enjoy their freedom but feel something may be missing. They may no longer accept the minutiae of their prior beliefs, but they long for some connection to them after a while. Their continuity and coherence in life just does feel quite right and they desire for continued spiritual growth. However, they do not know where to "hang their hats," so to speak. Reactivity and rejection give way in some to a longing for certain positive parts of the beliefs they have been avoiding.

This book will hopefully provide some signposts along the way for persons in either of the above categories or those in a mixture of both for they may need some assistance coming back to or evolving in their faith.

Breaking Attachments

Human beings are social creatures with profound needs of attachment.

When we break an attachment to another or even with beliefs, we usually suffer deep, emotional agony. Many dynamics may influence the extent of this suffering—how long the relationship has been in place, how important it has been, what our support network is like post-attachment, what we believe about the attachment, how many areas of our lives the break in attachment impacts, and so on. Therefore, we cannot always judge for ourselves how profoundly the breakup may impact us; much less should we judge how others react to a similar severance. A foundational principle in our dealings with people who leave particular churches or belief systems, therefore, should be that we not judge each other regarding the timing nor the amount of struggle involved.

Although people on similar wilderness journeys from toxic beliefs or simply beliefs that no longer can be maintained have much in common, complications vary enough that a simplistic "one size fits all" type of understanding will not be equally helpful to everyone. Each individual, no matter where in the process of an exodus, must assess carefully and walk by faith while being true to self as well as honest with God. One model for understanding the severing of an attachment to a church is that of divorce.

From working as a family therapist, I know from experience how varied reactions to divorce can be. People can usually expect a roller coaster of emotions during a marital breakup, often vacillating from shear panic to calm assurance that one can survive. Profound ambivalence is often present; people make emotional progress and then move back again. Clean, fast, simple, and easy breaks in attachments are unusual for caring persons, whether that break is with a spouse or with a church or even a belief system into which one has fully invested oneself.

If we continue with the model of divorce, think of a spouse who has an abusive partner and compare this relationship to a member of an abusive church. It may, in such cases, be very clear intellectually that one needs to divorce in order to survive emotionally and physically, but emotionally the person may feel confused. Often the abusive partner has used myths, much like the ones already mentioned in relationship to abusive churches, in an effort to convince the abused spouse that he or she cannot survive without him or her. The abuser may have told the victim such things as "You will never survive without me" or "No one would have you but me."

Cognitive Dissonance

There is a psychological term called *cognitive dissonance* that describes our internal tension and struggle when we simultaneously hold conflicting beliefs or attitudes or when our beliefs contradict our behavior. For example, if a person believes that divorce is wrong and honors the marriage vows but simultaneously realizes that staying in an abusive marriage endangers one's children or oneself, the resulting conflict is cognitive dissonance. The reality of the abuse may be clearly evident, but the intellectual belief about the permanence of marriage and the emotional attachment to the spouse may cause the person great internal struggle and confusion.

Or to take another example, one may change a religious practice out of a new understanding, but the old familiar pattern may result in the new religious practice feeling awkward for a while. Often when there is change in our beliefs, we go through a wilderness experience of emotional ambivalence before our minds and hearts are integrated regarding the belief. As the shattering of one's assumptions and beliefs gains in momentum, so does a shattering of the foundation of one's security or of life itself.

God may appear absent. Former friends may abandon or reject. If one is employed by the organization, career and income may be lost. Like an addict who goes into physical withdrawal, so a person leaving the attachment and womb of a religion, or deeply held belief system, often has emotional withdrawal. Some even return to their religious addiction or belief system that no longer really works in order to get relief. These people can be the saddest cases of all because the cognitive dissonance of such a return ensures that they have no peace—or they go numb to their spiritual experience and become robots going through motions of meaningless religious life.

There is a better way. The road best traveled is walking through the wilderness toward the promised land of healing. It is not an easy journey, and it is filled with dangers, but it is well worth the agonizing struggle of the wilderness to find the promised land of freedom and wholeness.

Considerations When Making a Theological or Belief Transition

Do not minimize the stress. In stress theory, there is the concept of a "pileup" of stressors, and I know of few instances where the pileup of stress is any higher than when exiting some churches. The stress is not just in one area of life but is pervasive across most domains of living. There can be horrific stress because of the breakdown of a person's support system; social network; family life; mental, theological framework; emotional securities; personal history; worldview, in some cases, financial and career investment; and so on. For a time, a comfort zone is nowhere to be found.

Even persons who are very stable can only take so much, and when stress is so intrusive to so many areas of life, there is much at risk. When you survey the wasteland you must cross to get to a better spiritual and emotional land, prepare as best you can and beware of these dangers and risks. Otherwise, you will certainly be blindsided by the wilderness temptations and confrontations. For many, it will not be a short or simple journey. I have known some who continued to feel guilty for years even though they knew for certain they were at a different point theologically and their former way was empty for them.

Guilt can be true guilt or false guilt. In cases such as this, one is not dealing with true guilt for a wrong done but with the residual effects of a conscience that has been carefully indoctrinated and is, therefore, overly active with a guilt that is false. I think this is especially true for those who were indoctrinated as children, so beware.

Those who have been simply reactive or rejecting of certain beliefs may not have such an upheaval returning to the positive parts of their beliefs but this process of sorting out what to welcome back versus what one no longer accepts as true can also be a difficult process.

Allow grief and realize that persons grieve in various ways— there is no one correct manner in which to grieve. When there is loss, grief is normal, not abnormal. Our society has popularized certain stages of grief, thus promoting a belief that if you go through the various steps, grief will be completed.

However, in real life, grief is emotionally all over the place and is rarely a neat progression of steps. It is so important not to expect a neat and tidy grief package and to remember that anyone who cares deeply may grieve deeply when there is loss. Grief reveals past attachment; and caring and will, most likely, wax and wane and subside for a while before coming forth with a new vengeance. Some grief lasts a lifetime; however, time normally does bring relief.

A person may experience some losses long after leaving a destructive church. For example, being part of a special group, the group identity, the apparent closeness of the group, the like-mindedness, and so on—although largely false perceptions—are powerful losses. The extreme cases of loss of family and friends can be traumatic; being cut off suddenly and dramatically can cause a questioning of trust and the validity of all relationships.

It is important to remember that those cutting themselves off from you are responding to their own insecurities and inability to tolerate anything that threatens their fragile belief structure. This self-induced separation may be the most obvious illustration of the bankruptcy of their religion at a deeper level. Truth is not so easily shaken and disturbed. The unfortunate reality is that many times there is nothing you can do to bring any closure to such relationships, and persons who do cut off in this manner often have to demonize you to give themselves an excuse for their behavior.

Don't let criticism and negativity overcome you; move toward the positive. One of the worst things that can occur is that we can take on the characteristics of our theological adversaries and become just as negative and controlling as they are. It takes grace to accept persons where they are, and it may help if we remember our own past and that we were in the same place at one point. One of the marks of psychological and spiritual maturity is the ability to move to a different understanding without rejecting those who remain at the former level of understanding. Your journey is yours and you have to find what works for you and what is meaningful and honest for you.

How to Survive Transition Trauma

Accept that ambiguity is much more a part of faith than you have previously been taught. There is not a clear-cut answer for every theological question we have. Questions and honest doubt are parts of genuine faith. Most toxic organizations have an answer to everything, but you have to accept their presuppositions in order to believe them. I am not sure where it originated, but the quote "Why is it that the religious institutions that say they have all the answers never allow any questions?" holds great insight. Ponder it. One has to ask if certainty in all areas is really valid or necessary. It appears to me that living with paradox and not being anxious about it is a hallmark of psychological health.

Put your focus on Christ and his acceptance of you and your journey. Christ accepted the disciples and shared communion with them shortly before they abandoned him. Their faith was imperfect and in transition, yet Christ accepted them and continued to work with them. He will do no less with you.

Christ is much more graceful than what you have internalized from the teaching of your toxic church. He is with you even when it doesn't feel he is, and he will bring you through the wilderness, for he has been there and knows the way.

Remember the importance of forgiveness, but acknowledge that forgiveness may not be immediate and may not bring positive feelings. Just as Christ has forgiven and continues to forgive us, so we seek to forgive others. But it may take time to forgive a religious institution that you feel has harmed you. Even when you choose to forgive, the hurt and pain may remain; forgiveness it not a magical wand that removes all negative feelings.

Our acceptance before God is not based upon the perfection or imperfection of our own personal forgiveness. If it were, our forgiveness would become a demand of salvation by performance. Ultimately, the only way we can forgive an entity that never apologizes is by turning over to God our "right" to get even. We are accepted, and God continues to work with us in that acceptance in spite of our continued imperfection in forgiveness or in anything else. Perfectionism is an example of the all-or-nothing, black-and-white thinking that sometimes remains with us from toxic religion. It is unrealistic, and God's grace reaches us even in the struggles of our daily lives.

Seek balance in all areas of life. Not one of us is truly balanced; and giving attention to the spiritual, social, physical, and mental areas of life is vital, especially when we are under stress. Do not neglect the importance of physical exercise to assist with emotional agitation and depression. Avoid extremes. Eat well and find outlets and hobbies that take you away from the intensity of the religious struggles to which you have been exposed in your transition. An obsession with theological issues without balance becomes an insane approach to living.

Take a long and meditative look at the foundational Christian concepts such as grace, forgiveness, acceptance, and God's infinite love. If you continue to study only minute details of obscure theology, your relationship with God will not develop. If you constantly feed on negatives, your faith will be starved. Most of all, you need to develop your relationship with Christ and find solace and healing in his care for you. Careful reflection on the great principles and concepts of Christianity will pay great psychological and emotional dividends.

Encouragement for the Journey

The chapters of this book are meditative signposts along the journey toward health engagement of the Christian faith. You can approach your faith anew and with a different orientation. Read the meditations and let them embrace you and help heal your soul. It is truly a myth that you cannot survive an exodus from a toxic church or even the transition from a long-held belief system that worked in the past.

There may indeed be emotional trauma as you make the break into the wilderness once you leave, but even Christ himself spent some time in the wilderness. The temptations of the wilderness are great, and the fierceness of the emotional predators that attack you can be devastating. However, once you have made it beyond the wilderness, you will recognize how Christ sustained you even during your weakest moments. You will wonder how you previously got so caught up in all the theological briars and thickets of the old system. You will begin to relish the newfound freedom to commune with Christ without all the distractions of a belief system that no longer works for you or a toxic belief system sticking and jabbing its sharp thorns into your psyche. Best of all, you will find that Christ is the Promised Land beyond the wilderness that brings rest to your soul![2]

EPIPHANY / NEW YEAR

This is the season of the Christian year that is associated with the manifestation of Christ and his message to others. It has to do with the revelation of God and with insight and a grasping of meaning. When we combine it with our celebration of New Year's Day, we can focus upon new revelations that may challenge and move our lives in new directions. Thus, the focus on New Year's resolutions and the love-hate relationship we have with them is because these concepts challenges us to move in new ways, but we resist. God's way can reveal new ways for us to move and also empower and give impetus for actual change. Epiphany/New Year is a basic signpost along the way to coming back to faith.

Epiphany/New Year

2

Arise and Seize the New Year on a New Journey of Faith

Preparatory Reading: Isaiah 60:1–6

There is a blessing that someone has made that goes like this: "May all your troubles last as long as your New Year's resolutions!" And we consider this a blessing because we really do not think New Year's change is truly lasting change.

However, may I suggest that short-lived change does not have to be the reality of our lives. If we partner with God greater possibilities can come to us. Think about it. Welcome to a time of reflection and meditation.

Prayer: Oh, God, we step with some trepidation into the uncharted territory of a new year. We do not know what to expect. We do not know what dangers are ahead. We do not know the way ahead. We do pause and ask for your guidance and direction as we begin this journey. In the spirit of Jesus, we pray. Amen.

Sometime ago, there was a newspaper story about a couple who were sitting with a marriage counselor for their first session and the counselor asked them to identify what seemed to be the root of their problems. The wife responded, "It all started when we thought it would be cute to think up each other's New Year's resolutions." You may be able to imagine the problems that could result if a spouse wrote down all the changes that he or she felt their mate should make! Don't try it!

It is a fact that we can often think about how other persons should change and how they could better their lives. However, how little time most of us give to considering that we might could better our own lives or improve the way we are.

How long has it been since you did an evaluation of your life to decide what direction you should go? How long has it been since you set some goals for yourself? How long since you attempted to grab hold of life rather than just let life happen?

Oh, I am very much aware that we cannot control much of life, but I do think we can make much more happen than we often do. Some of us are procrastinators and are always planning to do something next year or in the future. But what about now? This is the beginning of a new year—could not this turn of the year bring you the impetus toward something new in your life?

Football coach Lou Holtz once said, "If you're bored with life—if you don't get up in the morning with a burning desire to do things—you haven't enough *goals*." There is truth to that, is there not? Many people live with no goals that motivate them—that is, as if they have passionate goals at all. And if we have no real goals or if we keep putting off doing good things or making some needed changes in our lives, then things will remain the same. The time to move toward is now, if you want to reach your goals and potential. Life does not have to be status quo. Life does not have to pass us by while we are passively letting it happen!

Jesus challenged persons to look at themselves and to make drastic changes in their lives. We have somehow tamed Jesus and made him much less disruptive to our lives. But I encourage you this year to read the teaching of Jesus and note the challenges he places upon persons and upon us. There is no question in my mind, but that Jesus called persons to reach their full potential. He challenged them to work on the interior of their lives and let the spirit of God transform them.

Let me remind you of a few concepts Jesus promoted:

- He told persons they must be born anew—in other words that transformation must occur in their lives.
- He told persons not to judge others.
- He called all persons to love more deeply.
- He challenged the priorities persons had in their lives and for them to place the spiritual at the top of the list.
- Jesus called for persons to trust God totally.
- Jesus challenged persons to forsake that which was bad for them.
- Jesus greatly challenge those who saw themselves as religious to become more than they were.

On and on we could go, Jesus was not one who would allow us to be complacent and content with a mediocre existence.

We have a confluence of things occurring at this time of year. We are at the beginning of the New Year, and this is the church season of Epiphany. *Epiphany* means "something that reveals itself," and we think of this time as the revealing of God through Jesus. Jesus reveals a new way for us. He is a light shining in the darkness to show us the way. Do you need a new revelation for your life, a new direction, a new vitality about life? Do you need to see more than you have been seeing? Do you need to grasp more than you have been holding? Can you believe that there are new and vibrant ways of living that we can discover this year if we remain receptive?

When our children were young, we went as a family one Saturday to visit an elderly lady of the church. We had a good visit with her, and she appreciated that we came to see her. As we were leaving, we had prayer and she gave us some candy. In the car, afterward, I thought I was waxing eloquent as I shared with the children how important it was to help others and visit the lonely and so on.

Our son—as deadpan, innocent, and honest as a five-year-old can be—piped up and said, "I just go for the candy." What honesty! The captive audience for the teachable moment I thought I had somehow had been blown to bits! I have thought about that many times and wondered how often we get off track in life and just go for the candy or the money or the prestige or whatever our temptation may be. Maybe we all need to review our priorities from time to time. This may be the time to do just that.

A New Year's resolution is a solution to a problem or a way of fixing a problem in our lives—a part of which may be new directions, new insights, new priorities, or new goals. May I suggest that we allow Jesus to reveal himself to us and shine into our lives to give us direction for this New Year? We should allow Jesus to move us in new directions and to motivate us to new ventures in life. Find something to sink your teeth in to that will challenge you this year. Find a goal that will stretch your ability this year. Find a teaching of Jesus about relating to others and apply it to your life. Find a call of Jesus to interior life transformation and ask his spirit to lead you to be reborn.

Of all persons, Christians, should be willing to tackle big ideas, big changes, and big goals for we believe that God's spirit is willing to assist us in transformation. Maybe you do not fully believe such a statement, but it is true that if you don't put yourself in the position to achieve great goals if you are not open to new revelations in your life they will not often happen.

Now let us go to our lectionary reading for today, Isaiah 60:1, which states, "Arise and shine for your light has come and the glory of the Lord rises upon you."[3] These are marvelous words of Isaiah, written so long ago that we can apply to ourselves. What words of encouragement these must have been for the Hebrew people and what words of encouragement they can be for us!

"Arise and shine for your light has come and the glory of the Lord rises upon you." What would happen if we really got the concept that God is shining his light upon us, upon our pathway, upon our lives, and all that God reveals is rising upon us?

Isaiah looks to a time when God's light will shine upon the people. What an encouragement it must have been to hear these words so long ago and what hope they must have resurrected! What do these words do for you? "Arise and shine for your light has come and the glory of the lord rises upon you." Get up! Wake up! Get up from your spiritual slumber! We do not want to be a couch potato this year; instead, we want to arise and shine!

Light is ever the symbol for the presence of God. Can you begin this New Year with the thought that God is present with you? Arise and shine for God is present with you.

- Arise and shine for God will be present with you in whatever you face this new year on a new journey of faith.
- Arise and shine for God has something new to reveal to you as you come to new faith.
- Arise and shine for God will help you accomplish what you need to accomplish in this New Year on a new journey.

Are you willing to arise and shine and seize the opportunities of this New Year? It will pass, and you will be the same person as you are now unless you seize the opportunities for personal and spiritual growth that God provides for you. Therefore, my challenge to all of us at the brink of this New Year is to arise and seize the tremendous opportunities that God has placed before us for this year!

3

You Are Loved by God Can You Accept This Fact and Start Living by it?

Preparatory Reading: Jeremiah 29:11; Matthew 3:13–17

Sometimes we can be all around something and not know it. You have heard the saying: "if it had been a snake it would have bitten me!" Well, I wonder what we are passing by spiritually, I wonder what we are bumping into spiritually but we have not really seen it or experienced it yet. My thesis is that we are hearing without hearing. Think about it. Welcome to a time of reflection and meditation.

Prayer: Oh, God, we know and yet we do not know; we believe and yet we do not really believe. Somehow, through the miracle of your spirit, help us to really and truly experience your love this day. We pray in the spirit of Jesus who breathed you into his life as readily as he breathed air. Amen.

What if you could discover something at the beginning of this New Year that would revolutionize your life? What if you could find something that would change the trajectory, the direction, of your life? What if your life could be transformed in such a manner that it could no longer be the same? I am writing about a positive, energizing, and calming change in your life!

It is my understanding that a bumblebee, if dropped into an open tumbler, will be there until it dies unless it is taken out. It never sees the means of escape at the top but persists in trying to find some way out through the sides near the bottom. It will seek a way where none exists until it completely destroys itself. I think we often never find our way to happiness and meaning in life even when the route to meaning and happiness may be very near to us.

The Smith House in Dahlonega, Georgia, has been sitting on a gold mine for more than a century. During renovation of the landmark hotel back in February 2006, workers discovered the entrance to a four-foot-wide hole under the concrete floor in the main dining room. The hole goes straight down nineteen feet to the entrance to a gold mine under the building.

Captain Frank Hall built the house in 1899. The story goes that the city forefathers would not permit Hall to excavate for gold on the property because it was too close to downtown businesses and would create too much noise. It may be that he built the house to cover up his mining operation until his health failed and he sold the land. If the renovations in 2006 had not been done, the gold mine would not have been rediscovered according to Chris Welch, the owner of the hotel.

For many years, the owners had joked with patrons that they were "sitting on a gold mine."[4] They had no idea just how true a statement that really was. How often are we, as humans, sitting on a gold mine of opportunity and real life and we never truly discover it?

Are you going through life without really having anything to hold on to? Do you have no anchor and are, therefore, tossed to and fro? Do you have no root with which to draw nourishment day by day? Do you find yourself blowing with whatever emotional wind that comes along for the day?

Maybe your life is like that of Ernest Hemingway, the literary genius, who once said of his life, "I live in a vacuum that is as lonely as a radio tube when the batteries are dead, and there is no current to plug into." It is an illustration based upon the technology of his time, but you can get the point.

We move all around the truth that I want to underline and print in bold letters for you today. We know it at one level, but some of us do not experience it. Some of us have heard it with the ear but not with the heart. And it makes a difference which way we hear it. Some of us just simply do not believe it at a deeper level because of our pasts. We acknowledge it, but we do not really believe it. But it can revolutionize your life! It can cause a transformation in your experience of life and living. Is there something just under the surface of your life that needs to be discovered or rediscovered? Could you be "sitting on a spiritual or life-changing gold mine," so to speak?

Here it is the concept I want you to get hold of: Can you hear it? Can you really hear it? Can you accept it? Can you really accept it into your heart? The fact is that God cherishes you, no exceptions!

I heard someone on the TV the other day use a term I had never heard before. He spoke of a person walking in a "self-cherishing" manner. I thought, *What a great description, but what if we could walk in a "God-cherishing" position or "cherished by God" position or walk knowing that God loves us and cherishes us?*

Don't make any exception as to why God does not cherish you for that is false thinking. God cherishes you—no exceptions, no buts, no ifs—just the plain truth. God cherishes you, no exceptions. And you say "But I have done so and so" or you say "If only I would do such and such, God would love me" or "When I reach a certain level of spirituality, then God will cherish me." I say, "No, no exceptions. God cherishes you right now, this moment, no matter, no exceptions."

Now, have you really incorporated that into your being or has it been heard over and over but denied by you or never really grasped by you? Are you like the bumble bee flying all around the answer to save your life but missing it? God cherishes you, no exceptions!

Jesus comes among the crowd to be baptized. He comes as one of the multitude coming to John the Baptist. He is our great example, he is our model, and he walks up to John to be baptized. John is uncomfortable with this and says so, but Jesus is firm and tells him to "do it and do it now." Matthew has the heavens opening at the moment of the baptism of Jesus and what happens? A voice comes from heaven and says, "This is my son, whom I love; with him I am well pleased" (Matt. 3:17).

This phrase is an obvious allusion to Psalm 2:7, which brings Jesus into the royal line of the House of King David. But it is more, so much more, for I believe Jesus is representative of all of us and that this is the very voice that God wants us to hear about ourselves as well: "You are my son, you are my daughter, you are my child, whom I love and cherish. With you I am well pleased." Can you accept it? Or do you find yourself arguing with the concept? Don't deny it, don't refuse it, drink it into your consciousness and it will transform your life!

Some of you have heard it at a superficial level all of your life but never incorporated it into your souls. Some of you have been so bombarded by the concept of original sin and that you are sinners and bad that you cannot fully accept the blessing that God bestows upon you. Now please pause and hear this, don't just pass it off.

God is much more interested in accepting you than in condemning you, despite what you may have been told in the past! I think the way the church came up with and has focused on original sin and has been so condemning at times was to control persons, and it has done untold damage. In fact, God does not condemn you. He accepts you as his child.

Just remember that story of the prodigal son—the father never rejected his son. The son rejected his father, but the father never rejected his son. He continued to long to see him and fellowship with him. The father had a son who remained at home—in the church, if you please—and it was the same with him. He never rejected the elder brother who was always in the church but never fully appreciated the love of his father. For you see, my friend, God cherishes you, no exceptions.

Whether you are outside of the church and out of fellowship with God or if you are sitting on the front pew of the church every Sunday and out of fellowship with God, God cherishes you, no exceptions!

Can you accept that? If not, I challenge you to do an inventory as to what blocks you from this vital truth. What keeps it from being your experience?

There is something transformational about grasping this, and it could change your life. Think of what would happen if you started living as a person who is confident that you are cherished by God!

Do you desire to have a new life this New Year? Do you desire to influence others for God this New Year?

It can be done. It can be done. It can be done. It can be done, if we will truly start living as a people who know—really know—they are cherished by God, no exceptions. Can you believe it? Can you accept it? Amen.

4

In God, Find a Beacon of Orientation for the New Year!

Preparatory Reading: Psalm 40:1–10

A blank slate of a New Year is before us. What will you write upon it? Are you ready? Are you excited about what it can bring? Do you want it to be a year of growth and fulfillment? What do you really desire for the New Year? Now, many of you may not even consider this New Year a time of new opportunities, but it is—with God. Think about it. Welcome to a time of meditation and reflection.

Prayer: Oh, God, we dare not travel this weary world alone. We are stating clearly and categorically that we need you to show us the way. We are lost without you, and we need you anew in our lives. Come, sweet spirit, and direct our pathways. Amen.

Well, once again we have dipped our toe into a New Year to test its temperature. What will the New Year hold? Are we ready for a New Year? Does it mean anything to you to enter a New Year?

Okay, I still like the concept of New Year's resolutions, or New Year's goals, if you please. Maybe it's just that it gives me a convenient tool as an author and minister. I don't have to muster up too much energy to get you to at least think about New Year's resolutions even if you do not make them. At least this time of year is a call to evaluate our lives, and I can make good use of that as a pastor, don't you think? So, you cannot blame me too much for the emphasis I give this time of year.

And I like the quote by an unknown author, "Many people look forward to the New Year for a new start on old habits!" Does that apply to any of us? I bet it does. Many of us will simply continue on in the same, old bad habits and usual negative practices that maybe should be challenged or changed. Now if you argue "Well, I don't believe in New Year's resolutions," that is fine, but when do you believe in challenging yourself and changing or attempting to make changes for the better?

As most of you know, research clearly shows that the great majority of persons attempting to stop smoking try numerous times before they are successful. And it is not only smoking where we struggle with making changes and where relapse is part of the process. Relapse is normal with change, not abnormal as some have thought; and when it occurs, we should get back on track and try again and try again and again until finally the change occurs and we are successful. And, yes, I sometimes break some of my own New Year's resolutions before the first day of the year is done so I have to get back on track myself.

Work with me as I attempt to help us with a point in our lives when some of us may be more open to self-evaluation and change for those times do not happen often.

Look at the text I have chosen for today, Psalm 40:1: "To the director of music of David. A Psalm. I waited patiently for the Lord; he inclined to me and heard my cry." Well, most of us are not very good at waiting. Maybe this would have to be written differently today for us and say instead, "I or we waited *impatiently* for the Lord."

Today, in the day of instant messaging, if God does not respond to us in a nanosecond, we have moved on to something or someone else. If we are honest, it might go like this: "God, I don't really have time to wait for you. Will you just come and part this red sea in my waters of difficulties right now? God, I just don't have time to mull around while you work this out. Can't we just skip this preparation time? Come on, God, get moving." Does that seem familiar? Does that hit home? Do we realize how desperate and impatient we really are? But the psalmist *waited patiently*—how I envy that. Maybe that should be one of my New Year's resolutions; I don't know.

But notice, as the psalmist waits patiently, what happens? The Lord turned toward him and heard his cry. What a wonderful thing that is when are struggling and crying and we somehow know that God hears us. This is the God we have. Our cries do not really go unnoticed or unheard.

Look at the next verse, which I think is maybe very appropriate for us coming out of a tough year: "He lifted me out of the slimy pit, out of the mud and mire." Many of us had a tough year. There was not a lot of good news in some past years. Some translations put this verse this way: "He brought me up out of the horrible pit."[5] You may look on the last year as a "horrible pit" of a year.

Was last year a difficult time for you? Was last year a horrible pit of a time? Did it seem like your life was stuck in a pit or stuck in the mud or in a terrible spot? Have you been barely hanging on financially or spiritually or relationally or in some other area of your life? Does it seem like last year is just a blur of disappointments and failed dreams? Life can hurl some pretty big waves at us at times, and it is difficult not to get pushed into the mud and mire and feel like we will not survive. And with no way to minimize the true impact of our hardships, we sometimes can also end up there sitting in the mud, having a little pity party all by ourselves.

At the beginning of this New Year, God wants to lift you out of the mire and mud and muck and lift you up to higher ground! He wants to give you a hope and a future in which to believe!

Maybe, just maybe, God wants to give you some new goals and some new resolutions to help you move in a better direction. God wants to lift you out of your "stuckness." Maybe you have not been managing your life well. Maybe you have been putting your energy in all the wrong places. Have you come to the point to where you have just disengaged from life or from what used to give meaning for you? Have you disengaged from God? Have you disengaged from assisting others? Have you disengaged from having goals? Have you disengaged from following your dreams?

If you keep on struggling in the mud and mire, you will simply keep on expending your energy on that like an automobile tire spinning 'round and 'round in the mud and you will have no energy for the good things of life. It is amazing how much energy we humans can expend for useless activities or for things that actually keep us stuck in a rut. Maybe this is the year, you have decided you will break free from the shackles that bind you and the glitter that blinds you to the better things in life. Break free by the grace of God, break free!

And while God's grace is free, change in our lives may take a lot of work. We do not change easily; we need to state that over and over again. It may take a time of being patient and working hard and putting in the sweat hours to get to where we need to get this year. Discomfort may be a part of growth toward a positive change; get ready to face it and overcome it.

Notice what God did for the Psalmist: "He set my feet on a rock and gave me a firm place to stand" (Ps. 40:2b). From being stuck in the slimy pit of mud and mire of life to having a firm foundation and a place to stand. "He drew me up from the desolate pit, set my feet upon a rock, making my steps secure."[6] This is the way one version puts it. What a wonderful trade that is! What a difference God can make! And what a difference it will make in this brand-new year if we allow God to make our steps secure instead of continuing on and on in the pit of the mud and mire of life! Oh, there may be mud in life, there may be difficulties we may get mired down in maybe some desolate places this year; but if God makes our steps secure, we can get through them.

We need an anchor instead of "stuckness," if you please. We need an anchor instead of shackles. We need an anchor instead of being drawn into a slimy pit. We need a firm place upon which to put our feet, we need a solid foundation upon which to place our steps. We need something, someone to hold us when the waves come upon us. We need an anchor to sustain us when the going gets tough to keep us from getting mired in the mud of life, and that anchor is God. God will lead you during this New Year. Trust in God!

The next verse in this Psalm was greatly feared by some of the choirs where I have been a minister. I attempted to join them numerous times, but somehow, I could not make the cut to get into the choir! And the choirs were dreadfully fearful one of these days I would sing with them. And I have to say, that was a valid and legitimate fear for I cannot carry a tune in a bucket. But notice Psalm 40:3: "He put a new song in my mouth and, a hymn of praise to our God." Maybe there is hope for me yet! Well, actually and unfortunately, I don't think it is a promise that God will transform me into a great singer.

What I think it is saying is that God will put joy in our hearts and a good attitude in our minds. Our hearts and minds will be encouraged and enlightened by our God. We all need to find a song in our hearts this year. We need the positive encouragement that only God can instill within. For me, that happens as we have a purpose to our lives and a direction. Rather than wandering aimlessly, we have direction with God, we have a purpose, and we have a reason. Do you want to enjoy this New Year? Do you want to find fulfillment? Then find a purpose in life, find a cause to believe in, find a way to help others, and allow God's spirit to minister though you.

Yes, we have dipped our toe into the New Year. We do not know what it holds for any of us. But, my friends, we can go ahead and jump into the New Year with energy and enthusiasm and purpose because we have a God who can anchor and sustain us through it no matter what. He will give us a "firm place to stand" (Psalm 40:2b). Go forth into this New Year with courage because of faith in the kind of God you have! Amen.

THE LENTEN SEASON

The Lenten Season is a time of reflection and renewal and can build upon the foundations of Epiphany/New Years'. It is a time of focusing awareness on our humanity and mortality. It is a call to order our priorities rightly. It is observed during the forty days from Ash Wednesday until Easter. The great themes of humility, vulnerability, preparation, perseverance, self-discipline, and overcoming appear to me to permeate this season and provide signposts along the way back to faith in a more balanced manner:

- Ash Wednesday
- The 40 Lenten Days from Ash Wednesday until Easter

The Lenten Season

5

Ash Wednesday
Doing the Math
What Do You Need to Add
or Subtract from Your Life?

Preparatory Reading: Genesis 3:19

Funny thing is that spiritual dynamics do not always follow all of the normal ways we understand things. Sometimes, when we subtract or give away, we gain and sometimes when we add, we end up with less spirituality. Then, on the other hand, sometimes it works in the natural order and we add positive things to our lives and it enhances. Funny how it works. Have you ever noticed that? Think about it. Welcome to a time of meditation and reflection.

Prayer: Oh God, sometimes we get confused for we have been taught certain ways of doing things or our natural logic appears to suggest a certain way of living. But your way sometimes challenges us to move in new directions and new ways of living. Help us to be open to explore. Amen.

Let's do a little math. How many of you liked math or currently like math in school? Many of us find that when our children are in middle school (or even earlier), their math is too difficult for us. Will you be brave enough to do a little math with me?

Ash Wednesday makes us ask, Do I need to subtract something from my life that is keeping me from really living? Do I need to remove something from my habits to free myself to more abundant living? Do I need to let go of something to have a closer walk with God?

These are tough questions, but the math is not too difficult—simple addition and/or subtraction. Yet it may cut across the grain of our normal thinking and living. I attempted to be creative and turn the normal thinking on its head a number of years ago with a group when I suggested that we might not only consider what needed to be removed from our lives but what we might add during the season of lent.

I got in trouble with a church member because when I said that, the member was afraid the other spouse might decide to add a couple of more credit cards for Lent! However, I did not learn my lesson, so I still challenge us to think of not only what we might need to remove from our lives but what—and now I have learned to say it more carefully—"positive" thing can you add to your life that might bring you closer to God or enrich your life?

Ash Wednesday has traditionally been a time of penitence, and that can be the beginning of change. We search our hearts for those things that are holding us back and limiting our lives and offer penitence that we have allowed them to do so for too long. It is a time of being vulnerable for we look closely at ourselves on purpose, and sometimes it involves addressing our frailties and our mortality. The is the way we begin the journey of Lent in the forty days leading up to Good Friday and Easter. So, it really is the long road to Calvary.

It is about death and resurrection to the old; it is about dying to parts of our lives and being transformed; and it is about vulnerability for we realize our limitations. It is a time of recalling our mortality, and we are not living life to the fullest for most of us live like we will never die. As the Bible says, "For dust you are and to dust you will return" (Genesis 3:19b). This is to be a season of repenting of wrong, making things right with God and each other, and preparing for death and resurrection—not only to witness the death of Christ but our own fragility and death so that we will appreciate life and living more completely.

A guy up north who has had too much to drink decides to go ice fishing and he packs up his stuff and goes out onto the ice. He starts sawing a hole in the ice, and a loud, booming voice says, "You will find no fish under that ice!" The guy looks up, ignores it, and continues on. The voice repeats, "You will find no fish under the ice." The drunk guy looks up again and says, "God? Is that you, God, trying to warn me?" The voice says, "No, I'm the manager of this ice rink!"

The man who had too much to drink was looking in the wrong place for fish. I wonder how often we are looking in the wrong place for life and all the while we have been disoriented and pursuing it in the wrong places. Or have we been looking for God or spiritual truths in all the wrong ways and places? The Lenten Season is a time to get reoriented and redirected.

There are parts of us that resist such a journey since we do not really like to reorient and change and we certainly do not like to think about our own mortality. However, the reality is that we sometimes do need to realize that we will not spend eternity on this earth. And we need to prepare for a closer walk with God and for milking all the fulfillment we can out of life. And we need to realize some things do need to die in our lives and some things need to come to life in our lives.

What do you need to add to your life? More kindness, more love, more faith. Of what do you need to let go? Do you need to let go of an old, destructive relationship; a grudge; a hurt? Giving up caffeine or sweets may help in some ways and can be symbols of deeper issues, but why not also, this year, add something of eternal value or subtract something of only earthly value and really be transformed and be ready to be resurrected to new life on Easter morning? If we do the math correctly, the Lenten season and Easter morning could be the beginning of a new life for you and for me. Amen.

6

Knowing That God Is Pleased with You Opens Up All Kinds of Possibilities!

Preparatory Reading: Mark 1:9–15

Jesus was a voice crying in the wilderness of confusion about God. What did he say? What was his message about God? Have you been confused about God? How does your theology line up with the theology of Jesus? How does your belief about God line up with the belief of Jesus about God? Maybe you have missed something along the way? Could it be true? Think about it. Welcome to a time of meditation and reflection.

Prayer: Oh, God, we struggle with those who teach us to live in fear and anxiety and who condemn our every move. They present a different gospel which, as the apostle Paul writes, is really no gospel at all. But it has taken hold in so many parts of our world and it reaches out to grab hold of our souls. We pray for the discernment to hold on to your good news that frees us to great possibilities and great hope. We pray this in the name of the one who exhibited your good news to all persons, Jesus Christ. Amen.

We have now entered that season of the Christian year called the Lenten Season, that forty-day period leading up to Easter. It is initiated by Ash Wednesday; and this is a time of preparation, a time to prepare for the Easter celebration. However, we want to get it right at the onset.

The Lenten Season is not to cast great fear in our souls and resurrect all our anxieties about our morality in one short miserable period of time. This season is not to make us feel distant from our God but to bring us nearer to God. We may think of denial of certain things during this time, but it is not in order to gain favor with God but to help remove barriers that may keep us from a deeper spiritual experience.

As we are entering this Lenten Season, it is important that we have the proper understanding as we move deeper into it. How in the world can we begin to look more deeply at ourselves and to acknowledge—if not, embrace—the fact that we will not live forever? How are we to seek to deny ourselves without it becoming some kind of legalist performance we feel compelled to do in order to make God love us?

Well, there is something that is foundational, something we will not want to miss or we will get it all mixed up. There is something that should keep us from living in fear, and it should keep us from seeking God's approval or acceptance by our performances.

And it is right at the beginning of the ministry of Jesus as well, and we started laying the foundation with it in one of the earlier chapters we had on Epiphany at the beginning of the New Year and want to come back to it in more detail here. I do not think Jesus could have endured so well; I do not think Jesus would have had such great faith if he had missed this.

Here it is embedded in our text for today—don't miss it! Mark is not verbose. He gets to the point rather quickly. We preachers sometimes have been accused of being long-winded and not getting to the point. There was this lady who was visiting a church one Sunday. (Now read carefully or you will miss this.) The sermon seemed to go on forever, and many in the congregation fell asleep. After the service, to be social, she walked up to a very sleepy-looking gentleman, extended her hand in greeting, and said, "Hello, I'm Gladys Dunn." And the gentleman replied—thinking she said "I'm glad it's done," referring to the sermon—said, "You're not the only one, ma'am, I'm glad it's done too!" Sometimes, the message that members give is hidden in what they say. They are trying to be courteous, but their real feeling come out in the way they word things. A woman leaving church one Sunday told to her minister, "Pastor, it seems that every sermon you preach is better than the next one!" Think about that for a moment—she literally meant his sermons were getting worse each week!

A long-winded preacher was shaking hands with members of his congregation. In a slip of the tongue, one church member accidentally called him "Never*end*" instead of "Reverend." A man said, "Preacher, I really enjoyed your sermon today. It was like water to a drowning man." See how you tell us things you did not mean to say?[7] However, I am even getting long-winded with these illustrations so back to the text.

Mark speaks of the temptations in the wilderness much more concisely than the gospels written later. He simply has the statement "He (Jesus) was in the desert forty days, being tempted by Satan." No mention what the temptations were.

But before all that note, the key verse I want to point out for today—verse 11—and it is a message we tried to grab at the beginning of the year as well, but here we try to sink it deep into our minds again. Before Jesus was tempted, before he went into the wilderness, before he begins the Lenten journey—so to speak—these words are spoken. Don't miss them!

And do you know what I believe? I believe internalizing these words, "You are my son [or daughter], whom I love and with you I am well pleased," are absolutely vital in understanding the sustaining power and grace that Jesus had to endure and endure so well.

Jesus knew he was accepted by God, he knew he was loved by God, he knew that God was pleased with him. And note, this is prior to the great works that Jesus did. It was prior to his ministry. It is prior to all his good works for God. This is so essential. Do you get it? Jesus did not toil and sweat and labor and sacrifice to be accepted by God. He was accepted, he was loved, and he was pleasing to God from the beginning. And it is the same for you—this is the gospel, this is the Good News Jesus taught to us!

And the church and many Christians have it wrong and many dear persons have had it come to them incorrectly. Listen to these words that someone once gave to me. The person wrote,

> Everything about Lent takes me back to when I was little. It made me feel hopeless. It seemed like the only thing anyone cared about (especially God)—the only thing that mattered—was what you did wrong. It was called an "Examination of Conscience". Everything you did –every mistake, every act, as well as every thought had to be "reflected on"—meticulously rooted out, examined and specific sins identified. ... The warning and repercussions and threats about consequences were horrifying. I felt like the obtaining of forgiveness was impossible. I was never able to meet all the requirements.... Even now—Lent makes me feel scared, shattered, and not the least bit forgiven for all that I have done. I still feel like lightening is about to strike.[8]

That, my friends, is the result of legalist teaching and a performance-based, controlling, and condemning approach to God. I want no part of it for it has literally destroyed millions and millions of dear souls. It is not good news; instead, it is bad and awful news. It is anxiety and trauma producing, especially to persons with sensitive or overactive consciences.

And part of the problem is that things are backwards in legalism. In legalism, we have to have good behavior and performance in order to be accepted by God. Wrong! The gospel puts it the other way around and states we are loved and accepted by God, and then it calls us to seek to live rightly. Obedience is still called for, but it is not perfectionism and it is not the basis of our being loved and accepted by God.

Maybe you do not struggle like the person who wrote the quote I shared with you, but maybe you have no passion about your God because you are still in a legalist frame of mind. No wonder there are struggles with having excitement and enthusiasm about God, if our view of God is so distorted. However, once you really grasp the gospel—that you are beloved by God, that God is pleased with you, that your life can be radically transformed—then passion may swell up within your heart.

Don't you see that Jesus revealed to us that our mission is not to go around condemning people like many Christians have done and are doing. Our calling and our mission is to reveal a God who loves, a God of unlimited compassion, and a God who is pleased with and wants to approach all persons.

How was Jesus fortified for the temptations he was about to face? How was he prepared for the trials and tribulations of life? How was he prepared to give his life on the cross for righteousness and for justice? Maybe this passage will bring you to a new understanding.

This one statement is enough, we mentioned it at the beginning of the year and again at this time of entrance of the Lenten Season, and it needs to be repeated again and again: "You are my son, whom I love, with you I am well pleased" (Mark 1:11). Jesus heard that. Jesus got it. Jesus incorporated it into his soul. And it sustained him; it gave him hope in the midst of suffering and pain. It took him through temptation. It supported him through rejection and abandonment—even the abandonment of his own disciples.

And I do not think it too far-fetched to state that these words are the focus of his ministry, the summary of his gospel. They are not for him alone; they for all of us: "You are my son or my daughter, whom I love, with you I am well pleased."

Can you hear God saying those words to you this morning? They can transform your life. They can sustain you through great temptation and trial. They can give you unbelievable hope and courage. You are a child of God and God loves you. This is the message of Jesus, this is the gospel.

And we have distorted it and we have misused our distortion, and we have somehow given the concept that God is out to get us and catch us at every turn. And condemning churches have been sources of perpetual discouragement and fear. This is simply wrong and not the way of Jesus.

So, if you find yourself wanting to continually condemn and criticize, check out how unhappy you actually are in yourself and how unaccepted you feel and run to God to accept his acceptance of you and be transformed.

The Christian life is not one of gloom and doom. It is not a life of constantly fearing we will be rejected by God or constantly thinking that we will be sent to hell. No, no, no! The Christian life is instead one of unspeakable joy and hope because of our foundational belief and knowledge is that God loves us and is pleased with us.

"For God so loved the world," it says so in John 3:16. It does not say "For God so *hated* or *despised* the world" or "God so condemned." No, it states "God so loved the world!" God so loved you and me. That's it. That is the gospel! Can't you hear God shouting to you over all the noise of the world, over all the distortions of theology, that you have been taught? Listen to what God is saying to you: "You are my son, you are my daughter, whom I love, I am well pleased with you." Or we could translate it this way: "You are my beloved son, you are my beloved daughter, in whom I have found my delight."

Oh, my dear friends, realize how delighted God is with you! It will transform your life! Amen.

7

Journey into the Wilderness On the Tiptoe of Expectation!

Preparatory Reading: Mark 1:1–8; Luke 3:15

Are you ever at a crossroads in life? We all come upon them, maybe even more than we realize. Do you think that is ever true of you? Could it be that you are at an important crossroads, a fork in the journey of life, and you may or may not even be aware of it? Maybe you need a signpost along the way on your journey. Think about it. Welcome to a time of meditation and reflection.

Prayer: Oh, Lord you are blessing us in many ways, and we want to continue walking with you. Help us make the right choices, for they determine our destiny. May the call of John the Baptist provide direction of our lives this day. Amen.

Even a cursory reading of the New Testament will reveal that its authors hit religious people pretty hard. Actually, as I read it, religious types are condemned more than about any other group of people. Did you ever think about that? What is going on here? We have a book that tells us about Jesus, tells us about the struggle of God with humankind, and the struggle of humankind with God; and yet it blasts religious people out of the water. Now, of course, it could not be talking about us as it is talking about those who lived long ago. It blasts those who are stuck in their traditions but not us, of course.

Well, on the other hand, truthfully, it may apply to us for it is still true today that some blatant offenders recognize their need of help whereas, sometimes, we church people get complacent and self-assured, do we not?

We continue to explore the Season of Lent as it is a journey into the wilderness. You could call it the wilderness of the inner part of our lives or the wilderness of solitude and reflection. The wilderness it not a place we often go; it is strange to us. Yet in Biblical tradition and spiritual experience, the wilderness is important. Traversing the inner wildernesses of our lives with care is vital.

If we go out to the wilderness on this day long ago, we meet a rather strange person who wore clothing made of camel hair and a leather belt around his waist. In some circles today, particularly some creative and nonconformist types, John's attire would fit in very well. And actually, it was not so strange to the people of his day for the tradition of the prophets, those spokespersons for God who were usually a bit off the beaten track. We need to appreciate such people at times who challenge our status quo. Here is what I think is another slam at the religious bureaucrats of that day: We don't find the spokesperson for God speaking in the synagogues or even the city streets. He is outside the church of the day, even outside the city. I wonder why that is so?

Could it be, is it possible, that from within the synagogue—or what I will call in our context the church that the voice of God—could not be so readily heard? There were layers of tradition and ways of doing things that stifled the very voice of God. Could that be? And there are a lot of preachers today that always give the party line of their denomination. For some, it appears that it is more important to be the voice of the denomination than a voice of God. It is too easy to be a sycophant, a *yes* person, within the denominational hierarchy at times.

Well, the person we are looking at today was no party-line type of person. He is not a conventional person. He, along with his cousin by the name of Jesus, called persons to a way of transformation and change. They did not defend the status quo but called to new ways of living. I'm not sure that John would have been able to preach in any of our churches any easier than he could have been permitted to preach in the religious institutions of his day.

Mark says that John was a voice crying in the wilderness, telling people to "prepare the way for the Lord make straight the paths for him." It is my understanding that in ancient times, when the king would travel, his workers and messengers would go ahead of him to prepare the roads and make a way for him to travel. John comes in this tradition, making a way for Jesus who will soon be appearing to the people.

John is a voice preparing the way of the Lord. He is attempting to set it up where people will come to Jesus. Now isn't that in many ways what we are to do as a church? We are to prepare the way for the Lord. Prepare the way for the God to meet people and people to meet God. We come together to worship, and that is one important aspect of the church. But we are also to make the church a place where God can meet with persons and people can meet with God. What a wonderful and awesome thing! How do we do that—prepare the way for the Lord? What are the barriers to God coming to people and people coming to God today?

I have been attempting to think about this a bit: what barriers do churches put up that stop or hinder persons from coming to God? I hope you will join me in attempting to assess ourselves and understand any barriers we might place in the way of persons coming to God.

Notice that the scripture says that people flocked to hear John the Baptist (Mark 1:5). He was apparently preaching what people of the time wanted and needed to hear. What are people wanting to hear today? What are people needing to hear today? What can we learn from John the Baptist?

First of all, his teachings as well as his manner were different. John apparently was not afraid to take a different approach. He was, as I said, in some ways rather strange with his camel hair and leather belt. His message apparently was in stark contrast to the shallowness and formal teachers of many of his day.

Second, his teachings called for repentance and baptism. He called people to decision; to die to the old way and be born to a new way of life. "Repent, repent" was his message. He called for a response from people. The Essenes practiced baptism as a continuing ritual, John used it as a once-only form or symbol of purification. Baptism had been personal, but John administered it to others. He took some different approaches.

A disturbing part of his call to repentance is found in Luke 3:7–10 where he calls the crowd a "brood of vipers" and states that those who do not produce good fruit will be cut down. This is strong language for us today, and we don't have all that he said so maybe it even comes across stronger to us today. But note this: John is hitting the synagogue people, the church people, rather hard. They often appeal to the fact that Abraham was their father as a way to be assured they were in God's favor. But John blasts that practice and basically says "It doesn't matter who your mommy and your daddy are, it doesn't matter that you have been in the church for years. What matters is that you repent and that your heart is right and thus you bear fruit or show evidence of a changed heart."

Third, his teachings pointed to Jesus in verse 7. This was his message—the message of Jesus. It says in Luke, in the New English Translation, that John brought the people to the "tiptoe of expectation."[9] Some even wondered if he was the messiah, but he clarified and pointed people to Jesus.

Fourth, his teachings revealed his humility. In spite of his boldness and his confrontational style, John was humble and did not attempt to take any of the show from Jesus. He did not take the glory for himself but pointed to Jesus.

In some ways, John is not a bad model for us as we prepare the way for the Lord in this day in this place. We too must be willing take a different approach, we too must call ourselves and others to repentance and to a changed life that reveals the fruits of the spirit. We too must point others to Jesus and we must walk in humility before our Lord.

Now, let me come back to my introduction—are we are at a crossroads in our lives? Could it be that we are at a decision time in our lives? Maybe some of us need to make decisions even today.

Could it be that we are being faced with a decision of huge importance? Maybe we are on the verge of tremendous movement in our lives, maybe we are at the crossroads, maybe we are coming alive by God's grace. When is the last time you were "on the tiptoes of expectation"? Sounds like a neat place to be to me.

We could be at a critical time. Maybe we have done well with some life adjustments, but more challenges are coming if we allow God to continue what God desires. Change will not always be easy. Growth brings its own challenges. All of us will have to open and receptive to accommodating new things.

On the other hand, listen to these works by an unknown author:

> The moment one definitely commits oneself, then providence moves too. All sorts of things occur to help one that would never otherwise have occurred. A whole stream of events issues from the decision, raising in one's favor all manner of unforeseen incidents and meeting and material assistance which no man [or woman] could have dreamed would have come his [or her] way. Whatever you can do or dream you can, begin it. Boldness has genius, power and magic in it. Begin it now.[10]

That is moving by faith. We will not always see the way clear. However, God will provide if we will but continue moving! We may be moving forward and doing great with the movement in our lives, but we cannot stop now! Let's move. Let's grow. Let's assist hurting people. Let's open our hearts to others.

The question is, How much are we willing to allow God to use us? Amen.

8

What Are You Avoiding on the Journey? Detours Can Be Dangerous

Preparatory Readings: Matthew 4:1–11

There are many powerful paradoxes in life. For example, it has often been found that people who know they are dying often begin to truly live. But it doesn't have to be that extreme. The paradox can be that we somehow come to truly find authentic life and find God in the wilderness places of our lives. There is a richness of life to be mined in the desolate, lonely, painful, and barren wilderness trials of life.

Often, if we search for such precious treasures and find them, they will change our lives and we will cherish them for the rest of our lives. What wilderness places are you avoiding that could be a route to God and a more authentic life? Think about it. Welcome to a time of meditation and reflection.

Prayer: Oh Lord, you amaze us for your ways are not our ways. You use what we would not use. You transform what we count as of no value. But Lord, please perform your miracle this day and may we begin this day having been blessed by your spirit. Amen.

Out of the Darkness
Out of the dark forbidding soil
The pure white lilies grow.
Out of the black and murky clouds,
Descends the stainless snow.
Out of the crawling earth-bound worm
A butterfly is born.
Out of the somber shrouded night,
Behold! A golden morn!
Out of the pain and stress of life,
The peace of God pours down.
Out of the nails—the spear—the cross,
Redemption—and a crown![11]

In our scripture passage for today, we have Jesus being led to the wilderness. As the door is opened to the ministry of Jesus, he has the great blessing of the baptism, and then he has the trial and temptation of the desert. He is given a special blessing of God's spirit, and then an evil spirit confronts him with great temptations.

Here we have Jesus entering not only the desert, but he is also entering deeper into human experience as we said in the previous chapter. Jesus is not distant from what you and I experience; he has been there. He knows of our trials and temptations. He knows of the desolate and lonely places in our lives. Isaiah 53 is often applied to Jesus, and verse 4 says, "Surely he took up our infirmities and carried our sorrows." In fact, it says he was "a man of sorrow and familiar with suffering" (v. 3b) and that "he was cut off from the land of the living" (v. 8b).

Jesus is familiar with the barren deserts and wildernesses of our lives. He has been there. There are times in life when we feel barren and empty inside. The choking dust of the whirlwind of troubles makes it difficult to breathe, and every step is heavy and full of emotional pain. At times, many have known the reality of Psalms 89:18, "Darkness is my closest friend." Have you been there? When were the times when you could say "darkness is my only companion"? Are you making that statement now?

There are times in our day-to-day lives when it is all miserable darkness and threatening shadows, aren't there? Trials and difficulties and temptations come to us all. Note that these special trials of Jesus come after the high day of his baptism. Mark does not record the specific temptations as Matthew and Luke do.

This makes me think that there we numerous temptations, not just the three. But Jesus faces special trials after his baptism. Baptism is not some kind of spiritual vaccine that protects us from trials and temptation. In fact, it can be that following special blessings, we are more susceptible to the difficulties of choosing the authentic life.

The deeper authentic life does not just happen. Although we often don't want to hear this, somehow, trials can be turned into a route to the deeper life. What about the wilderness spaces in your life?

Maybe you have had a great loss and you are in that no-man's-land of grief and loneliness. The grief floods over you and you feel you cannot survive.

Maybe you are stuck in a dead-end job and cannot find a way out. The monotony is killing you. Maybe you have been greatly disappointed in a relationship or even with your relationship with a church or a group of believers and you struggle to get your footing in the midst of feeling abandoned and disillusioned. Maybe you are in some vast spiritual wasteland, struggling and wrestling with God as Jacob did of long ago. Your spiritual life feels barren and dry. Whatever our struggle and trial, there is hope, for sometimes the thing that almost destroys us has the potential to give us new life.

I was visiting with a church member once, and I asked one of those questions that I have a reputation of asking: "How has having cancer changed your spiritual life?" With absolutely no hesitation, the person replied, "It has enriched it."

"It has enriched it." Wow! You see, sometimes we are better because of what we have gone through. This is not so easy to see in the midst of difficulties, but later we can often look back and realize it. Sometimes, we go deeper only when we are pushed and weighted down with the trials of life. Can that be?

One of the things I believe with all my heart is that for the Christian, things are not always as they appear to be! We have hope. Not some otherworldly, sugarcoated reality denying stupidity but real hope. Jesus said, "In the world you will have troubles, but take heart, I have overcome the world" (John 16:33).

We are heading for the Easter celebration. Easter is hope. It is reported that Goethe wrote, "Sometimes our fate resembles a fruit tree in the winter. Who would think that those branches would turn green again and blossom, but we hope it, and we know it."[12]

Therefore, for the Christian, the dichotomy about the wilderness is not so crazy for the desolate, barren, lonely, devastating areas of life often become our meeting place for the holy. We somehow can become more open and receptive to our God in the desperate places of life. But it doesn't happen if we avoid the rough places of life. Sometimes, we have to walk through the barren places to find the openness to receive our Lord. Sometimes we have to keep our feet moving even as we say "Darkness is my only friend."

Therefore, if your back is against the wall and you are overwhelmed and at the end of your rope—don't despair. For God may use this time to deepen you, give you new opportunities, and bless you. Jesus desires to walk with you in the wilderness places of your life, he has been there and waits to meet you there. Amen.

9

Temptation The Seduction of Power

Preparatory Reading: Romans 8:26

There are times in life when it is difficult to sing. During such times, about all we can do is make a little whimper or even only make a groan. During such time, we don't know how to pray. During such times, according to Romans 8:26, "The spirit helps us in our weakness. We do not know what we ought to pray for, but the spirit intercedes for us with groans that words cannot express."

In times of difficulty, have you had any words you could not express? Well, take heart. The spirit can even make known groans to God. I don't know about you, but for me, that's good to know. Think about it. Welcome to at time of reflection and meditation.

Prayer: Oh, God, we don't always have nor can we find words to adequately express our struggles or our pain. Therefore, we ask your spirit to be our spirit and communicate for us. Amen.

As we are traveling, anticipating, and longing for the Easter celebration, we have been taking the necessary journey through the wilderness as we continue walking through the Lenten Season. Before the authentic life come trial and tribulation and testing; before the promise land comes the wilderness; before victory comes the battle; before resurrection comes death.

The wilderness can be a desolate, barren, and lonely place. It can be hot and dry and cold and freezing at night. We all have our own wildernesses. Those difficult and tumultuous deep valleys of life where negative and apprehensive thoughts stalk us like breasts of prey. We feel alone, and the darkness is so thick we could slice it with a knife. Trials beset us, and we are tempted to call it quits. After all, What's the use? Why go on?

When we try to do the right thing and then we see those who could care less about what is right prospering, it makes us question. Maybe all this loyalty and authenticity stuff is only for the weirdoes. Maybe the end justifies the means, and we should just compromise a bit to get there. At times, it is really, really difficult to hang on in the wildernesses of life, isn't it? It is especially difficult to hang on when God seems absent.

There is a wonderful and comforting text that is tucked away in Hebrews 4:15b. Notice, referring to Jesus, it says that he "has been in every way tempted like we are." Christ experienced the temptations we face. He has been there. He groans within and at our pain. And, you know, the good news is that Christ has not only been there, but He promises to be with us in our times of trial as we face the wildernesses of our lives. The wilderness can blossom forth with the birth of a deeper experience with God for he meets with us in the wilderness in a special way.

Now it is a fact of humanity that most of us want to take a detour around the wildernesses of our lives. We may even see the promised land in the distant future, we may see ahead some wonderful goal in life, but then we see the wilderness between the promise land and us, so we run in the opposite direction.

My friends, there are times in life when we have to take the route through the wildernesses of life—times when we have to face our fears, face our demons, face our limitations, and walk right into them. The promised lands of life may be slow in coming; they may take discipline, self-sacrifice, and involve risks. However, faith often has to be exercised in order to develop and grow. Where are your wildernesses? Your wildernesses are the desolate, lonely, and difficult places you need to traverse to get to a better place.

Jesus did face temptation, as the book of Hebrews says, and we find his temptations spelled out best in the passages of the story of his temptations in the wilderness. The story tells us that Jesus was tempted to be a baker instead of a healer, feeding people's bellies instead of their souls. He was tempted to give bread that satisfies taste temporarily but would not be the bread of life. Jesus responded by the wonderful words "Man [*humans*] do not live on bread alone" (Matt. 4:4). There is more to life than the physical.

When I was growing up close to Chattanooga, there was one of those places where you could go to an all-you-can-eat buffet called B's Restaurant. I don't know if it is still there are not. Have you ever gone to such a place? Somehow, such places promise more than they can deliver. Somehow, even if the food tastes great, by the time you have made sure you are getting your money's worth (and that is such a good excuse to overeat), you are beginning to feel miserable.

We are tempted to believe that surely a person can certainly live by eating at B's Restaurant alone. But it is not true. A person does not live by eating at B's Restaurant alone. Eating is necessary and enjoyable, but somehow there has to be more to life than that. Life needs balance.

Then in this passage, we have the tempter coming to Christ and offering all the kingdoms of the world and all authority and splendor. Not a bad offer for a poor peasant; maybe even more enticing than food. Not a bad offer, if you want the end to justify the means. I mean, if Jesus was ruler of all the kingdoms of the world, he could force all to worship him, could he not? But, of course, I hope you recoil at the placing of *force* and *worship* together even in the same sentence and certainly know that Jesus would have no part of that.

However, in reality, down through the centuries, the temptation of Christians and other religious folk to force others to believe their way can be a human tendency. Unfortunately, there have even been times when those who disagreed with certain other Christians were beheaded or burned at the stake. This was done by those who also called themselves Christians but may have believed differently and desired to maintain the status quo. Some of us are thankful that Christians are not burning at the stake today. However, in some areas of Christianity, they may not literally burn at the stake but you certainly can get emotionally and psychologically burned. You see, the old adage that "power corrupts and absolute power corrupts absolutely" is true even in the Christian faith!

There is something very wrong when religion uses coercion and force to have its way. Religion and the power of force are a fearful mix; we see it in the world today. It can sound so tempting. All the right language can be used—concerns about values and concerns about our society—and, suddenly, the call to be forceful initially appears to be the way to go. But is this the way of Christ?

There is a very large difference in a religion that has power versus a religion that uses power to coerce. You see, there is wonderful power in Christianity—the power of the spirit. But our power is not by force but by humility; not by coercion but by invitation; not by control but by example; not by domination but by service.

There is a wonderful sermon that was preached by Martin Luther King Jr. entitled The Drum Major Instinct.[13] In the sermon, he uses the example of James and John at the last supper where they ask Christ if they could sit on his right and left when he came into what they thought would be a political kingdom. Martin Luther King Jr. describes the desire for recognition and importance as the "Drum Major Instinct," something we all have. Then he goes on to describe how destructive this can become.

Listen to part of what he said:

> And the church is the one place where a doctor ought to forget he's a doctor. The church is the one place where a PhD ought to forget he's a PhD. ... The church is

the one place where the lawyer ought to forget he's a law-yer. And any church that violates the "whosoever will, let him come" doctrine is a dead, cold church, and nothing but a little social club with a thin veneer of religiosity.[14]

We are not to lord it over each other in the church. We are not to have moral arrogance or feel moral superiority. For there is a great danger in spiritual overconfidence and feeling we know what is right for everyone else.

Martin Luther King Jr. goes on in the sermon I referred to and says,

> And so Jesus gave us a new norm for greatness. If you want to be important—wonderful. If you want to be recognized—wonderful. If you want to be great—wonderful. But recognize that he who is greatest among you shall be your servant. That's a new definition of greatness.[15]

So, evil would have us believe that greatness and power and authority come by taking control, but Jesus turns this on its head and refuses this kind of power and instead continues in the role of a servant.

Dwight L. Moody once said, "The measure of a man [*or woman*] is not how many servants he has, but how many men [*persons*] he serves." When our daughter was nine years old, she had some buttons and a shirt that said the words "Girls Rule" on them, and it was cute. But if Christians have a slogan, it should not be "Christians Rule" but "Christians Serve." True greatness comes from service. No force, no coercion, no shaming, simply people responding to needs and out of their love for God and wanting to be a part of what is happening!

There is yet a final nuance to this particular temptation of power and dominion and control that I want to point to. It is subtle but very real. Again, it has to do with rushing things and not doing them in God's way. It has to do with control. Many in the Christian

Church are not willing to accept that salvation is by grace alone. For, you see, that appears to leave us out of the picture too much. We add a little of our own works and depend upon ourselves for a little insurance that we make it.

We can end up measuring our eternal destiny and ourselves by how well we perform or behaviors we do or don't do. It is subtle, but it can be a worship of our own good works and our own abilities. It is a false religion, it can replace worship of God alone, and it can lead to insecurity, or, on the other hand, a "holier than thou" attitude.

Paul and the Christian scriptures are very clear that our acceptability to God is not based on what we do or don't do. Our acceptance before God is based upon God's grace and love. We are totally and completely accepted by God. No matter who we are or what we have done, no matter how many times we have blown it or blow it, the good news is that God accepts us as his children and will never throw us away. Therefore, we serve God not in perfection but with the desire of our hearts to respond to his goodness to us!

Therefore, when you are in the midst of temptation and in the wildernesses of life where darkness abounds and nothing appears to rescue you and there is little to hang on to, never forget that God in Christ is lovingly looking at you through the darkness and nothing in all creation or in heaven or in hell can separate you from that kind of love and care. You see, you don't even have to be a drum major—it is enough that your heart is making music to your God, even if it is a sob or even only a groan. Amen.

10

Temptation
Risking Too Much for the Wrong Reasons

Preparatory Readings: Luke 4:9–12

> What are you willing to risk for your faith? Does faith call you to do heroic acts or sensational acts? Actually, the same act can be an act of faith or an act of presumption. Think of the Israelites and the Egyptians at the Red Sea. Both took the same steps and risk of walking into the sea, but the reasons they took the first step were quite different. For the Israelites, it led to salvation, but for the Egyptians, it led to death.[16] God does call us to take risks, but what kind of risks is he calling you to take? Think about it. Welcome to a time of meditation and reflection.

Prayer: Oh, God, we are thankful that Jesus walked the way before us and has pressed down many of the painful thorns of life so that our way can be easier. Amen.

We have come to our concluding meditation on our journey into the wilderness during this Lenten Season. We started by first making sure we heard the voice of God as it came to Jesus and affirming him. Just as we need to be affirmed in order to make it through the wilderness, we then followed the people going out into the wilderness to see a rather strange person whose clothing was made of camel's hair and called forth a message to repent. His name was John the Baptist. We followed Jesus into the wilderness to be tempted and tried.

As we noted, a time of vulnerability and testing appears to often follow a special experience such as Jesus had at his baptism. And we said that Jesus, by going into the wilderness, was also entering in a more profound human experience for the wilderness can be a lonely, barren, and desolate place. We all have such places in each of our lives—places of special testing, lonely places, places where we are tempted and tried. However, we have also said in this book that the Biblical tradition presents another side of the wilderness. So it is not only a place of spiritual struggles; the wilderness can, on the other hand, be a place of spiritual growth and closeness to God as well.

Jesus was tempted, tempted to be a baker instead of a healer. He was tempted to be politician and use political power and force instead of the power of the spirit. He was tempted to politically rule instead of humbly serve.

Today we want to think of the last temptation we find in the passage we are studying. By the way, Matthew has the order different, so we do not need to get hung up on what order they came in but note the lessons to be learned from them. Personally, I think they are illustrations or grouping of many additional temptations Jesus faced during his life and that we face. And we know that temptation did not stop for Jesus; they dogged him throughout his life as they do us.

Now we come to our key scripture for today: "Do not put the Lord your God to the test" (Luke 4:12). The main point here is that Christ shows us that we are not to put God to a needless test. God does not normally change physical and natural laws for the Christian. If I decide to walk out in front of a Mack truck, I will end up flat as a pancake. If I want to play Superman and leap over or off tall buildings, gravity will still work and I will come in for a rather abrupt landing.

There are sincere persons, we find as examples and we do not condemn them as persons, only their mistaken beliefs. There are persons up in the hills of Tennessee who consider snake handling an exhibition of true faith in God.

By the way, this sermon is *H* rated. *H* for heavy. At least, for me, we will get into some heavy issues, or maybe you have resolved all of these for yourself and it will be simple to you, I don't know. Anyway, for me, it is *H* rated, not *R* rated, or we would probably have more people here!

Fred Craddick tells the story of a minister who, years ago, had widely advertised a sermon entitled "What's under the Bed Sheets?" and tells that there was a huge crowd that came out—people standing in the aisles, people standing up in the back. When the minister got up to preach, two men rolled out a blackboard with a sheet in front of it. They lifted up the sheet, and there was the sermon outline. Needless to say, there were a lot of disappointed people![17]

But back to the snake handlers. They are "true believers" in the sense that Eric Hoffer uses the term.[18] *They will not look at any evidence that their belief might be mistaken.* And there is good evidence that the practice is not a very good one—snake handling, that is—for many have been bitten and died.

Notice that in this story, what Satan is proposing is not much different than proposing snake handling. In fact, maybe he would have proposed snake handing if he was not sore, a little sensitive, that he has been called a servant or snake himself! He chose another suggestion of putting God to the test. "Jesus, just take a little leap of faith off the temple—you can even play a little hopscotch off the temple and the wall of Jerusalem, if you would like. God has said he will have his angels fly by and catch you so you will not be harmed.

"Don't you trust God, Jesus? Come on now, Jesus, where is your faith?" Can't you just hear him saying "Jesus is a chicken, Jesus is a chicken"? "You say you believe, now prove it! Just a little leap of faith, and we will make this salvation complex of yours happen more quickly. The Jewish people anticipate the messiah will put his foot down in Jerusalem. They will recognize you as the Messiah if you just put God to the test."

Now, let me ask you, Do you believe God has promised to protect you and keep his angels around you? Many of us took such concepts in with our mother's milk. Many of us could even point to biblical texts about God keeping charge over his people.

I was teaching a Sunday school class for youth a number of years ago. Jonathan was a sixteen-year-old, all-American boy. He had been raised in the church where his parents were elders. Jonathan was a good, young man. He came to church and participated in my class one Sunday. I received a call late Tuesday night of that week that Jonathan had died. He had played some basketball—shot some hoops—and then later told his dad he was feeling tired and started up the steps to his bedroom, then turned to his father, and said "I love you, Dad. Good night" before he went on up the stairs to bed. He died of a genetic heart condition during the night. Sixteen years old, in church on Sunday, dead on Tuesday.

Jonathan's parents had always prayed each day for God to protect and watch over their children, but one died during the night. Does God protect his people? Even Satan is quoting scripture in verse 10. Or, better yet, should we have faith that God will protect us? Are we at the mercy of life, just like everyone else?

Fact is, we all live in denial about how vulnerable we all are. There are no guarantees about our life continuing. Now, I don't think we should sit around and think about death or morbid thoughts all the time; but we should, on the other hand, be realistic. But the real question again is, does God protect us in some special way?

That is one heavy thought of this lesson, but hold on, I have a double barrel today. The second shot at you asks the question, "Is it wrong to put God to the test?"

Well, Deuteronomy 6:16 says, "Do not test the Lord your God." First Corinthians 10:9 also says "We should not test the Lord." Then, of course, we have our scripture reading for today with Jesus saying, "Do not put the Lord your God to the test."

So how do we avoid needless testing of God and yet move forward in faith, leaning on God to work in our lives? After all, isn't faith a sort of putting God to the test and trusting that he will do his part? Does anyone want to volunteer at this point to finish this chapter for me? We seem to have walked into quite a predicament. Tough questions.

I think I will stop now. Reminds me of when I was five years old. I had a part in the Christmas program, a poem or cute saying to say. I walked up to the front, stood hands on hips and looked out over the audience, and then without saying a word, walked to my seat and sat down. The audience roared with laughter. So, I have this history of just stopping, Maybe, I should do it again, only I somehow don't think you would laugh.

Well, what about doing something like Abraham did who went away from his homeland because he thought God was leading him? He went by faith and he had to depend upon God—that was a sort of testing of the faithfulness of God. What about if we as Christians moved forward by faith in ventures we believe God is leading even though we might not have the money or resources for the venture at the time? Would that be okay, or would that be a perversion of faith?

You see, my friends, I believe there is a vast difference between tempting and testing God in the sense of some cocky attitude that we will prove that God exists. Some needless test to give a show of faith is not acceptable. However, when we are seeking God's will and believe that he has given us a directive to move in a certain direction. We can move forward in faith, testing in the sense of depending and expecting God to be with us.

In fact, I think God would welcome us moving forward in a humble way by faith. God wants to do more for us than we expect as churches and as individuals. At times, he waits for us to make the first move!

If we act based upon what God has shown he wants, then we are exercising true faith. Fredrick Buechner wrote,

Faith is better understood as a verb rather than a noun as a process than a possession. It is on-again-off-again rather than once-and-for-all. Faith is not being sure where you are going, but going anyway. A journey without maps.[19]

We are attempting to provide a few signposts in this book for the journey, but we cannot map it all out in detail. Faith is action oriented. There is a huge difference between simply, needlessly testing God and testing God in the sense of depending upon God on our journey. An excess of unreasonable trust can be presumption. We are not to be stuntmen and stuntwomen for God but men and women of faith in God. We are not to deliberately put ourselves in danger for needless show, but we are to risk all for Christ if we are called to do such.

God does not promise to protect the Christian when the Christian has a false sense of security and does dangerous things needlessly. The laws of life are not changed for us. To bring it a little closer to home, the Christian cannot drive ninety miles an hour, even when doing the lord's work, and expect to be protected by God. The Christian cannot ignore the body's need for exercise and expect to stay physically fit. The Christian cannot impulsively spend money and expect to have financial means.

Let me take it a step further. Most of the time, God does not intervene in natural laws, even when we are not being presumptuous. So, Jonathan, the young man I mentioned above, can die in the middle of the night at sixteen years old. Christians can fall and get injured. Christians can get sick.

However, I still do somehow—and I cannot fully explain it—believe that God, at times, does intervene because of our prayers. I think we should pray for the safety of our children and ourselves. God does intervene, but he doesn't have to. And we all know stories of bad things happening to good Christians, so we are not exempt. There are not absolute guarantees of protection, but there are absolute guarantees of staying with us. Even when bad things happen and we go through the wildernesses of life, God promises to be with us. That is enough for me. That makes it worthwhile even though I may groan and complain when bad things happen to me. Knowing God is with me at all times by faith is the thread I hang on to.

Therefore, there is a perversion of faith that needlessly tests God by deliberately doing crazy things. Maybe that is not such a temptation for most of us. Most of us will never purposely handle snakes to test God, and if you have a need for that, please don't do it around me.

But maybe, the real perversion of faith to which we are more likely to succumb is that we do not move forward when God calls us to move. Maybe our perversion of faith is staying too safe and not stepping forward as God calls us? What is God calling to you? Are you responding to his desire for your life? Are you responding to his desire for you? To use the words of Jesus from our scripture today: "Don't put the Lord your God to the test"—perhaps, by ignoring God's call upon your life.

Amen.

THE TRANSFIGURATION

I have included a meditation on the Transfiguration because the story offers lessons for us on the journey of faith and our seeking to awaken from our slumber to a more dynamic faith. And it also reveals that our faith cannot be static and locked in at one point in time.

The Transfiguration

11

The Mountaintop and Valley Experience on the Journey of Faith

Preparatory Reading: Matt. 17:1–9

Can we freeze our spiritual experiences and keep them forever? Can we simply carefully wrap our faith and put it in the deep freeze and keep it forever in a safe place? Does spirituality grow by being frozen or by being challenged by the red-hot suffering and pain of humanity? Think about it. Welcome to a time of meditation and reflection.

Prayer: Oh, God, we have plugs in our ears so that we do not hear you. We have distorted views of what is means to follow you; we have blinders on. Unplug our ears and restore our sight during the Lenten Season so that we can truly hear and see you as you really are. We pray in the spirit of the one who heard and saw you clearly, Jesus Christ, Amen.

We go about our daily lives, and we get distracted. We forget. We ignore. We fail to listen, and we forget God and forget what God is like. These meditations can be a time of getting to know God again a time of remembering what we have forgotten, a time of remembering the God we have forgotten!

Do you recall that on the first Sunday in Epiphany, at the very beginning of the year, when you read the story of the baptism of Jesus? Do you remember what we heard God saying to Jesus, we heard the voice of God speaking of Jesus, saying, "This is my son, whom I love; with him I am well pleased." Today we note that these words come again; they are found only at the baptism in Matthew, and we now hear at the transfiguration the same words to Jesus "This is my son, whom I love; with him I am well pleased."

Mathew is emphasizing that Jesus is the new Moses and that Jesus is greater than Moses. In Judaism, mountains are symbols of the divine and human meetings, and so in our text for today we have a mountaintop experience.

Jesus took Peter and James and John and took them with him to a high mountain by themselves (Matt. 17:1). Now we miss something if we do not see that Matthew is elevating Jesus as the second Moses and the new Moses and the one above Moses. The scene we have in our scriptures is reminiscent of Moses taking Aaron, Nadab, Abihu, and the seventy elders with him to Sinai: "They had a vision of God, and they ate and drank" (Exod. 24:11).

Have you ever had a mountaintop experience? Some of us have experienced moments when the barrier between the divine and human seems to be removed in some way and we experience the presence of God in some profound manner. Have you even had a mountaintop experience with God? Do you ever desire such an experience? By the way, the Christian life is not a mountaintop experience all the time—it has its hills and valleys and gullies and ruts and mud holes and bogs and swamps, as well as mountaintops. Let those who say the Christian life is always a mountaintop tell that to Jesus as he is being flogged or being nailed to the cross!

Notice what it says in Matthew 17:2: "There he was transfigured before them. His face shone like the sun, and his clothes as white as the light." I cannot explain this experience. Madeleine L'Engle writes of this story as moving beyond fact into myth.

> And don't let the word myth be upsetting. In one dictionary a definition of parable is myth. Far from being a lie, myth is a way for us to see beyond limited fact into the wonder of God's story.[20]

You have your way of understanding such passages as we have today, but they are beyond our usual understanding. They are beyond the literal, and they are more powerful than that. Was it a miracle that occurred on this mountaintop? Certainly, something extraordinary happened on that mountaintop. But the greater wonder, in some ways, is the transformational service that it calls us to down in the valley.

Perhaps on the mountaintop Peter wants to freeze the moment. He wants to build a monument to the moment (v. 4). He wants to pour concrete and set up steel beams and have this experience locked in so it will not escape. I sometimes wonder if that is what we have done with the church. We have built great structures to God and comfortable places where we think we can tame God and contain God, and by the very act we are making a God of our own image, one that is safe and secure instead of majestic and unpredictable.

How often do we want to contain our religion in safe walls and less threatening locations? Let's secure ourselves in this holy place, let's shelter ourselves, let's not be bothered by the poor and needy—they simply disrupt our comfort—they may make us look bad. They may leave their trash around the church and clutter it. They can be annoying. Let's keep our church clean and spotless by keeping such persons away. And if we ever get to that stance, we will also be keeping God away as well.

Now notice where I find humor in this story. Notice verse 5 where is it referring to Peter. It says, "While he was still speaking." Peter is droning on and on, running his mouth because of his anxiety and note that God interrupts him. We have all these teaching on good communication about not interrupting people when they are speaking, but in some cases persons have to be interrupted, and here God interrupted Peter. I find humor in that.

Soon, Jesus and the three disciples had to come down off the mountain. Even if you have a mountaintop experience, you cannot stay on the mountain forever. Mountaintop experiences do not last forever. There is other work to be done. There are needs in the valley. We cannot build a monument on the mountain and remain there. We cannot isolate ourselves from society as some have attempted to do. We have to go down into the messy valley of life and minister there.

Joan Chittister puts it well:

> Real religion is not about building temples and keeping shrines. Real religion is about healing hurts, speaking for and being with the poor, the helpless, the voiceless and the forgotten who are at the silent bottom of every pinnacle, every hierarchy and every system in both state and church.
>
> Real religion, the scripture insists, is not about transcending life; real religion is about our transforming life.[21]

And as Jesus and his disciples come down the mountain, it tells us, in verse 15, that they were met by human need. Jesus came down from the mountaintop down from dazzling brightness and light and became involved in the darkness of human pain and suffering. Don't you see how practical this is? Don't you see the message for us it contains?

We are to have our mountaintop experiences, but they are not to isolate us and become a rigid, protective barrier to keep us from real life. Any mountaintop experience is to prepare us for service and to come to the great valleys of human need and the great depths of human suffering.

I hope that you and I can have mountaintop experiences with God as we go through the days of holy week. I hope the time will be transformational. I hope it will prepare us for Mt. Calvary and for the trials of life and the sufferings of life. We need such experiences with God to prepare us for the journey ahead. Amen.

HOLY WEEK

Holy Week involves the events surrounding the death of Jesus and leading up to Easter. It has tremendous power to illustrate or give a microcosm regarding issues of life. We can see ourselves and humankind in the events that occur; we can see ourselves in the challenges and perturbations that are revealed about humanity. Loyalty and betrayal, depression and joy, brutality and gentleness, despair and hope—they are all illustrated for us to witness. The journey this week can give us signposts (showing us what we should avoid and what we should embrace) along the way on our own voyage of faith:

- Palm Sunday
- Holy Week
- Maundy Thursday
- Good Friday
- Easter

Holy Week

12

Palm Sunday The Steadfast Focus of Jesus During the Ups and Downs of Life

Preparatory Reading: Mark 11:1–11

Do you like a good parade? Do you like the natural highs of life? We all know that parades do not last forever, we all know that highs of life are limited as we saw in previous chapter. How steadfast are we through the ups and downs of life? There is something to be said for those who can remain steadfast and loyal in all that life throws at them. May I suggest that this is the way of Jesus and that he is with us in all the ups and downs of life? Think about it. Welcome to a time of reflection and meditation.

Prayer: Oh, God, even now as we are in a place of peace and comfort, we realize a little about how fickle we can be. We love the life of ease and we despise difficulty. We struggle when we realize how your way of peace confronts our arrogance head on and challenges us to live another way. Help us this day to find the way of Jesus for our lives is our prayer in his name. Amen.

Have you ever noticed what I would like to call the "roller-coaster syndrome of life"? By that, I mean how life can take you up at one moment and drop you down at the next. Life can be a series of plateaus where every event is pretty humdrum and is followed by a great fall into the valley of difficulty or by a rise to a mountain of exhilaration. Fortunately, most of the time, life is a valley that is not so low and a hill that is not so high that it wears us out, but extremes do happen.

As a minister, I experienced this to a small extent every week. I would get energized and excited about preaching, and then after I preached, I would feel depleted and down in an emotional and physical valley. Therefore, you could not depend upon much conversation with me after church.

However, in various situations, we can experience life in a very happy manner one minute, and later we can be in some type of depletion or despair. We get our paycheck and we are up, and then one moment, we realize it is already spent and we despair. We are excited to meet someone, but they don't seem to be interested in meeting us and we feel rejected. We plan to attend a special fun event, then bad weather comes, and then it is delayed and we are disappointed, especially for those of us who remain children at heart. We see this roller-coaster syndrome happen especially all the time with little children. They can go from great emotional happiness to crying their eyes out in a nanosecond.

Most of us who are older have learned to ride life out and recognize that what goes down comes back up and that we cannot stay on the mountaintop forever and will come down at some point. Perhaps, sometimes, we are also burnt out and fearful of the roller-coaster syndrome and shut down in a protective mode and miss out on really experiencing life. I have heard it a thousand times, "I don't want to get too happy because something bad is going to happen," or in another form, "I am walking through life with my guard up because something bad always happens or is going to happen." Do you ever do that? Is that your pattern of life? If so, you are missing out on a lot!

As we walk through this very important week in the life of the Christian heritage, I hope we will notice again, and in a deeper way, the balance that Jesus had in his life. He was steadfast in the ups and downs of life. He did not avoid the difficulties and calculated dangers of life, but he did not allow the danger of living to dampen his experience of joy and happiness. It is those who are open to all of life and living that experience abundant life.

Shutting down to protect ourselves may be okay for a short period of time, but if it becomes chronic, it numbs our happiness along with the pain we are trying to avoid. However, notice with me this week that Jesus lived life to the hilt. He did not avoid living his values in the face of danger, and he did not resist having a good time. If you have an image of Jesus as a strait-laced do-gooder who never had a smile on his face, you are mistaken. Jesus was steadfast in the ups and downs of life, and we should model our lives after his example.

On Palm Sunday, there is joyful celebration and excitement as Jesus comes into town according to Matthew, Mark, and Luke after the pattern of Zechariah 9:9, and part of that phrase goes as follows: "Rejoice greatly … your king comes to you, righteous and having salvation, gentle and riding on a donkey, on a colt, the foal of a donkey." It was one of those "up on the mountaintop" times in life. It was a parade of sorts, and everyone likes a parade, don't we?

Many put their own assumptions on what the parade meant. Jesus is going to lead us to overthrow the Romans. Jesus is about to announce his political aspirations. Jesus is going to bring us prosperity. Jesus is going to give us freedom. Jesus is going to heal our land. Jesus is going to turn us back to God. Jesus is going to get rid of all the false religious people. Jesus is going to take my side in the theological debates.

The people saw Jesus coming into town and knew the story of Zechariah and were excited. Some were looking for a Jesus who would be like whatever they wanted in life. The wanted a Jesus who would fulfill their desires whatever they were.

If Jesus were to ride into your town as a king, what would you desire of him? What would you expect? Would he find the same assumptions and expectations today as back there in Jerusalem? What do you want from Jesus? What do you expect from Jesus? What kind of Jesus are you looking for in your life? What kind Jesus would you go to see in a parade?

Would you like to have him come in military might and destroy those who disagree with you? Would you like for him to set others straight? Some today seem to want a Jesus of military might. Would you want a Jesus who forces all to do what you want?

Would you like for him to fulfill all your dreams? Some today seem to want a Jesus who is a Santa Claus with a load of material goods. What kind of Jesus would you go to a parade to see? What kind of Jesus would make you wave palm branches with gusto and spread your coat on the highway in front of him?

Jesus comes in a manner that is unusual for us today—riding on a donkey. It is a model of humility. It is a model of a different way of power. He modeled a different manner of exercising influence. He modeled the way of a different kingdom. Jesus modeled a kingdom that was not one of force and military might and coercion.

Now, don't you think that Jesus had some sense that the majority of those who lined the streets on his entry into Jerusalem would not be found when he got into a bind? Don't you think Jesus knew that when life put him down in a valley on its roller-coaster ride that most who were there on the mountaintop experience would not been found to offer support in the valley? But Jesus doesn't allow the fickleness of the crowd to distract him from this mountaintop experience. Jesus was able to remain steadfast to the present moment and milk it for all it is worth. He did not avoid happy times because he feared bad times. Jesus lived life to the hilt and experienced all of it. As we go through this Holy Week, that is exactly what we see.

We all like the mountaintops, we all like the parades, and we all like the celebrations. But what happens when hardships and difficulties come? Where are we found at such times?

Are you with Jesus today on the mountaintop? Are you at the front of the parade shouting "Hosanna, blessed is he who comes in the name of the Lord!" I think I see you now waving your palm branch, and there you are spreading your cloak on the street to pave the way for Jesus. It is an exciting time, isn't it? What are you anticipating from Jesus? And you are there at the head of the parade taking your place with Jesus for all to see. You are committed to him and loyal to him and praising him. After all, it is Palm Sunday of all days.

We are on the mountaintop. It is a good time. It is a time of celebration. But as we come to realize that Jesus is coming as a king of a different kind than we have imagined, as it dawns upon us that Jesus calls us to a different kind of kingdom—one of gentleness rather than force, one of peace rather than war, one of humility rather than arrogance—what will we do?

Will we go from the mountaintop to the valley of despair? Will we go from high stepping it at the front of the parade to slowly slipping away to follow another way, to find another parade? Will we leave and end up on a parade to nowhere? Maybe we will go to find an easier way that doesn't demand so much. As Jesus approaches the cross, everyone leaves him, even his disciples abandon him.

Where will you be as Jesus walks through this Holy Week? You have walked with Jesus on the mountaintop. Will you walk with him through the deep and dark valley? Or will you also go away? There is something to be said in favor of loyalty. Or perhaps you have been on a parade to nowhere and now you see that the Jesus's parade has substance and depth so you decide to be in Jesus's parade wherever it may lead you. Amen.

13

A Fragrance or a Stink—
the Contrast Is Clear[22]

Preparatory Readings: John 12:1–12

> Does the church ever cause you a problem? Or more specifi-
> cally do church members ever disappoint you? Please allow me to
> whisper a little secret with you: The church is made up of you and
> me, therefore, we cannot expect perfection! However, the church
> can be a pretty good place when functioning at its best and can
> be a teaching environment even when not doing so well. Think
> about it. Welcome to a time of meditation and reflection.

*Prayer: Oh, God, some of us have this love-hate rela-
tionship with your church. We admit that we struggle with
it at times. But we believe it has a lot to offer for it teaches
us about your grace. Bring your grace into our lives by way
of the church this day. We pray in the spirit of Jesus. Amen.*

I am going to make some of you mad at me. In this short
chapter I do not have long, but I bet I can succeed at making you
mad at me. I have a few negative things to say about the church.
Now, let me preface my statements by saying that I love the church

and have given much of my life to it. But I am going to talk a little about the church.

That being said, let me share with you a quote that I ran across years ago by Robert McAfee Brown where he quotes an ancient manuscript. Listen carefully to what he writes about the church: "The church is something like Noah's ark. [*So far so good, but here comes the kicker.*] If it weren't for the storm outside, you could not stand the smell inside."[23] (And by the way, have you ever wondered what they did with all the mature in the ark? If you figure that out, let me know.)

He is saying something about the stink in the church. Are you upset with me yet? Often we—and I include myself in this desire—so much want to think that those of us in the church—shall we say, uh, well—give off a better odor than those outside the church. And yet, in reality, we at times have our problems and bad smells in the church, do we not?

As I read this passage of scripture, I thought it brings home the point pretty darn well. One character, Mary, is creating a beautiful fragrance and the other, Judas, is creating a stink. Now maybe it is only a few churches that have some people creating a stink from time to time, but I think not. And if we are honest, we must admit that we have these two dynamics and characters in the church even today—saints and sinners—do we not? Are you with me?

Sometimes those of us who are ministers think we could have a great church if we did just did not have any church members, and sometimes members think they could have a great church if they did not have to put up with ministers! But truth is, we are all in this together and that is part of God's miraculous design of the church.

At times, we have yet attempted to present a different image to the world and pretend we are better than we are, and the world has seen through our facade and called us phonies. But the scriptures are more realistic, more genuine, and more honest; and they present the truth of the good and bad among the followers of God. The scripture even tells of one stinker among the inner circle of Jesus; and he is greedy, deceptive, and dishonest. In other words, he stinks to high heaven!

I am sure that you—as I—have had the experience of stepping into something a dog left behind, and pretty soon you have a certain aroma pervading your car or your house or even a group you are in and you wonder what is smelling and you look down to your shoe and you discover what has happened, to your dismay. So, you realize it is no wonder people were moving away from you! Well, sometimes we have people in the church "who step in it." We have to admit that, don't we? Of course, it would never be you or me! It is always on the other person's shoe!

But the other character in our story, Mary, is of a different sort and is worshipping Jesus in genuineness and adoration and openness, and she pours out perfume that begins to fill the house. And the church has some of the most fantastic people I have ever met and they add a fragrance to life that is wonderful. Maybe that statement will make some of you a little less mad at me.

Therefore, the church has both good and bad smells. The church has never been lily white and never will be; the church has not been without some kind of stink, and it never will be. What do you think of people who say they have never had any difficulty of any kind in their marriage? Those of us who have been married very long raise our eyebrows for we know the struggles of living with another even in the wonderful institution of marriage—and even if a marriage is made in heaven, it is not lived there.

Relationships can be messy and sticky and stinky. And in the church, we struggle with relationships but that is part of the growth potential in the church. If the church was truly perfect, who among us could join and who among us would be able to bear our souls to one another and admit our sins? This is not an excuse for problems in the church but a call for us to be genuine and open and honest about our struggles. Let's be honest. Yes, sometimes we do "step in it"—so to speak—in the church.

And let me zero in a little more. Years ago, Keith Miller wrote these words:

> Our churches are filled with people who outwardly look contented and at peace, but inwardly are crying out for someone to love them… just as they are—confused, often frightened, guilty, often unable to communicate even with their own families.[24]

Are we so caught up in looking good and putting forth a good image that we are shutting off those who need to reveal their pain?

Now, I am not saying that we have to necessarily hang out all out dirty laundry or share our stench, but maybe we do need to be more real in the church about our struggles.

We are at the doorstep of this most holy of weeks. As we progress through this week, we will see the contrasts among the faces around the events of the week and around the cross. We will witness those who, like Mary, open up a fragrance that makes us feel good about humanity and that call us to a deeper faith. On the other hand, we will see those who create a stink and those who create an odor that is not pleasant and we will be repulsed as we are with Judas in this passage.

But if we will be honest and if we will look closely, we will—as I believe it was that old preacher Clovis Chapel once said—"see ourselves in the faces along the road to Calvary and at the foot of the cross."[25] And if we look even more closely, we will see the good and bad in humanity, both among so-called believers and nonbelievers. If we really focus even more closely, we will see the good and bad, the good smells and the odors within ourselves and our own hearts. We will see that we are on a journey toward wholeness but we are not there yet and we will be humbled, and therefore, some of the self-righteousness and criticism in the church will have to cease.

Especially, as we witness our messiah, our savior, and the demeanor he maintains throughout this week and even upon the crude cross, we will be humbled. We will smell the sweet aroma of his purity and authenticity and genuineness. We will witness the fragrance of his compassion, even for his enemies.

Please allow me to challenge us this week to look more closely at ourselves to see the good and the bad, to note the fresh scents as well as the pungent odors in our hearts. There is an opportunity this week for us to take in more of the fragrance of Christ into our souls. By the grace of God, let's do it!

I believe Mary's act of releasing the perfume was a microcosm or maybe a symbolic act of how the fragrance of Jesus would be released into this world a little later. She anointed God's anointed. She pours the perfume on his feet, not his head, as a preparation for his burial. Her gift was extravagant as the gift of Christ to the world was extravagant. He did not contain himself or save himself just as Mary did not seek to contain or save the perfume. Her gift was poured out as his life was poured out. Just as the fragrance of the perfume filled the house just, like the fragrance of a crushed rose, the fragrance of his love filled the world when he was crushed on the crude cross.

Can you not begin to take in the sweet aroma of his gift to you? Can you not begin to smell the fragrance of the love and grace of Jesus for you? The fragrance is beginning to blow this way and will become more intense as we walk the pathway to the Easter this week. May we go forth to fill our lives and our churches and our communities with its fragrance—his fragrance. Amen.

14

Maundy Thursday What an Example for the Journey!

Preparatory Readings: John 13

> Relationships are so vital to our life energy and happiness. How do we do in relationships? How do we do when relationships are in a rough spot? What did Jesus teach us about relationships? Think about it. Welcome to a time of meditation and reflection.

Prayer: Oh, God, help us to love one another with some of the love with which you have shown us and with the love you have for us. In the name of Jesus, the lover of others, we pray. Amen.

What an example Christ is to us of how to live! What an example for how to be in relationships. Across the board, humans have difficulty with relationships—in families, parents and children, siblings, marital partners, friends, certainly enemies have relationship problems, in the workplace, in sports, and, yes, as we have already written, even at the church. But Jesus reveals to us some principles of how to love one another. In fact, at his last meal, he gives us a new mandate, a new commandment. By the way, the word *Maundy* of *Maundy Thursday* is from the Latin word for mandate. And it is from the mandate that Jesus gives in John 13 to love one another as he has loved us.

And on this night long ago, he told his last stories at a meal. The passage has some parallels to the passage we often study on Palm Sunday where Jesus had his disciples go ahead of him to make arrangements and he had made some contacts beforehand. On this night, he sent a couple of disciples ahead of Jesus and the others to make preparations. He needs a place that is secret and safe for he knows that his time is short and there are forces moving toward his arrest and eventual death. As the darkness is falling around them, a greater darkness is enveloping the heart of Jesus and weighing upon him.

I like the pure honesty of the gospel of Mark, which is the first gospel that was written and therefore the closest to the time of the death of Christ. Mark does not have a need to remove the humanity of Christ as some of the later writers appear to do. He speaks of the time a little later on this night when Jesus was distressed and agitated and deeply grieved—"Almost unto death," it states. This was not an experience that Jesus just breezed through with no intense feelings and emotional pain.

Jesus was a storyteller, and he was a person who liked to be at meals. Over and over again, he is at a dinner or banquet or talking about a dinner or banquet or food. In some respects, we could say that Jesus was killed because of the way he ate.

Sometimes I wanted to choke my children because of the way they ate. Children's table manners may be poor—and we know some of the sounds and burps that some children make at the table at a young age—but it was not the poor table manners that we could consider that got Jesus killed; it was with whom he ate that got him killed. He often found a way to eat with sinners and outcasts. His inclusion caused much wrath; and his inclusion of others, even sinners in some ways, contributed to his death. But this very thing reveals to us the way Jesus was in relationships. He accepted people.

He loved those who were difficult to love. And isn't that the key to all relationship—acceptance, warts and all?

What an example! What a dinner companion he must have been. What a storyteller! And on Maundy Thursday we remember his last dinner and some of his final examples and his final stories, many other stories we probably do not have. However, a man's final words should be heard. And he speaks to us from his final words long ago, from his final acts, from examples he gave at the end of his life.

He invites us to his last meal as well. He did not demand that his table friends forget their lives or ignore their world in order to dine with him.[26] And he does not demand that we forget all our concerns or ignore our stressors as we come to be with him or that we have it all together. We too are a mixed bag of mixed emotions and mixed confusion about living rightly. Yet he is willing to have us come to the table. He is willing to include us. What a powerful example of including persons, all persons, even us. And he "celebrated each of them" and he celebrates who each of us are. There was profound acceptance in Jesus. Again and again, Jesus ate with those whom others would avoid and exclude. His table was very large indeed! What an example!

He reveals it oh so clearly on this night when his disciples are not concerned about him—they are too wrapped up in their own little petty concerns—and they miss the opportunity to care and be in relationship with Jesus. They must have reflected on this oversight over the remaining years of their lives. But Jesus is even in tune with the one who will betray him and does not exclude even him. He is in tune with the disciples, as weak and faulty as they were. And his loves them anyway and he, as you know, even washes their feet as a servant. He is not afraid to get his hands dirty for those whom he loves. He is not afraid to stoop low for those whom he loves. He is not afraid to humble himself and put himself in a low position for those whom he loves. What an example!

And then he gives the clincher. He says and gives the mandate to his disciples. He gives the new commandment. And it is like a cannon shot from the mountaintop. It is like a clap of thunder in their ears. It is like a horrific explosion in their minds. He has set the example by his actions, he has grabbed their attention by his act, and now he is saying to them, "As I have loved you, so you must love one another" (John 13:24b). Do you see it? He is telling them, "You are to love *as* I have loved you!" Wow! What an example! Amen.

15

Good Friday The End Is the Beginning!

Preparatory Reading: Psalm 23

> Do you ever want to just give up? Sometimes the struggle of life becomes just too great, and you look at the world and ask, "What is this world coming to?" You hit the wall with your own problems of life and a little voice inside of you says, "Why don't you just give up? It's no use." If you are feeling that, I remind you that God is aware of your struggles and that God cares deeply for you. Think about it. Welcome to a time of meditation and reflection.

Prayer: Oh, God, come into our confusion and orient us this day. We get lost in a morass of disappointments and trials, and we lose our way. Bring us back to the beacon of your guiding light in our lives this day, we pray, Amen.

I want you to consider this reality today: Others have been where you are if the feelings I have written above are yours. This day, we remember the confusion and despair of the disciples at the time of the arrest and crucifixion of Jesus. Events of life somehow, at times, also bring trauma upon us, and we are confused and challenged in the depths of our beings.

There was a prayer at the end of a Sunday school lesson one day which included the words I am about to share with you. It was entitled A Prayer for Those Perplexed and Afraid, and I do not recall who wrote the words but it in part read,

Oh, God, help me to remember: that people of faith are often more confused than certain, more afraid than brave … you accept us with all our doubts and questions, with our faults and fears.

Do you ever need such a prayer in your life?

The disciples needed this prayer on that Friday long ago, and may I say that Jesus needed this prayer? Remember that Jesus asked that what he was about to face be taken away if possible.

Jesus comes to this point in his life, and his dearest friends—the ones with whom he has walked and talked for at least three years—have fled from his side. The people have mocked and jeered and sneered and laughed at him. He has been whipped and spat upon. He knows aloneness and rejection and abandonment and betrayal.

He is taken and roughly nailed to pieces of rough wood. His heart and head are pounding as they pound spikes into his flesh. But he stood for truth and honesty and love and compassion, and he doesn't give them up to save his own skin. He is true to the end.

The worst part for Jesus was not the physical pain. The worst part is the soul pain and the darkness that came upon him as he hit the emotional depths of humanity. We have sayings and even Biblical verses that sum up the truth of such times in life such as the following: "The darkest hour is just before dawn"[27] and "Weeping may remain for a night, but rejoicing coming in the morning" (Ps. 30:5b).

Jesus was at the darkest hour. Jesus was at the time of weeping. And for the disciples, it was the same—it was the darkest hour. For the disciples, it was a time of weeping. And we too at times come to the darkest hour of life, and we too come to the time of weeping. Maybe some of you are there right now.

However, being at the cross and being there when they crucified Christ is not the end of all things. The darkest hour is just before dawn. Weeping may remain for the night, but rejoicing (or joy) comes in the morning.

There are many paradoxes in Christianity and probably none greater than the fact that the end is somehow the beginning. We come to darkness this evening. We are surrounded by it; we are enveloped by it. But on Sunday morning, the end will become the beginning, and darkness will give way to the celebration of Easter. Can you hang on until them?

When you hit the wall in life and your world is shattered, can you somehow remember that "weeping may remain for the night, but rejoicing [or joy] comes in the morning" and that "the darkest hour is just before dawn" and that with Christ sometimes the end is not the end but the beginning? This is the hope that sustains us in the midst of the utter darkness of the Friday of the crucifixion and at any other emotionally gut-wrenching time in life. This is the great God we serve. Amen.

16

Good Friday The End Is Not the End!

Preparatory Reading: Matthew 27:45–46

What an amazing week is Holy Week! We can find ourselves in the characters of the week and we can see some of the issues our lives play out to one degree or another during the week. Holy Week teaches us about life and about ourselves. Think about it. Welcome to a time of meditation and reflection.

Prayer: May we see parallels that assist us in our daily lives in this most holy of weeks. May we witness the way through the darkness and have the fortitude to keep on keeping on. We pray this in the name of the one who endured until the end, Jesus Christ. Amen.

I never liked the TV programs that would come to the close and, on the screen, you would see the "To Be Continued…" sign. Do they still do that? It leaves one hanging in midair with nothing to grab hold to. Well, unfortunately, life can be like that as well, and we can have things that are not complete or that leave us disturbed. But if we will wait often, the light breaks through. This meditation is a "to be continued" meditation. It is not the end, and it is not over at the end of this chapter. There is more to come. However, for this moment, I would like for us to imagine what it would be like if this was the end and there was no more to come. Can we imagine that? Can we tolerate that, even briefly?

This meditation is to be continued, and if you miss Easter Sunday, you will be in great trouble and despair. Don't stop here. Read the Easter meditation soon! It is vital that you do so.

I have written of the emotional roller coaster we find during the Holy Week. Today is the bottom, the depth of the ride. Today is the deepest despair. Today, we drink the dregs of bitterness and find no relief if we remain here much like if we stop in life at some points, we will be in despair. However, new days do come! All this actually parallels or is a microcosm of life, isn't it? We all have disappointment, we all have despair, and we all have times of disillusionment.

The disciples were in the deepest depression and fear—they fled from their closest friend. They betrayed the best person they had ever known. They were cowards when their friend needed them, and then they were so ashamed as well for he had been tortured and killed.

But we also have to consider the utter despair that Christ experienced. It was horrifically hurtful that his disciples did not remain loyal to him. He was abandoned by those who loved him and mocked by those who hated him. He was beaten, spat upon, and ridiculed. He who had loved all and treated all with grace was treated like a criminal. There was no respect for him. There was no mercy for him, he who had invited all who was excluded and cast outside the city to a lonely hill of crosses.

Remember his words of despair: "My God, My God, why have you forsaken me?" (Matt. 27:45). Those are not the words of a contented person or a person with hope. They are words of profound despair, and they were the words of Christ and sometimes they are our words. They may even be your words today.

They did not originate with Jesus as they are from Psalm 22 that he repeated; however, they fit his experience. And they fit the experience of all persons in despair from the beginning of time.

Who among us has not uttered those words or ones similar to them—"My God my God why have you forsaken me?" They are the lot of humanity in this world. They are the bosom buddies of depression and disillusionment. There are times in life when God seems absent. There are times when there is no God whom we can find.

One thing I like about Christianity is that is it real to life. This week of Christ's is very much a pattern we find in life. It is much more profound for obvious reasons, but it is our experience to some degree as well. Life is not always good—it has it losses, its abandonments, its empty and lonely times. Despair is common to our lives at times.

Think of such times in your life. When were you at your lowest? When were you the loneliest (and we are all lonely at times)? Didn't you cry or feel like crying, "My God, my God, why have you forsaken or abandoned me?"

There is a darkness that comes over us at such times, and we feel we cannot survive. There is no hope. The sun is blotted out. The thunder roars in our heads. The tears sting our eyes, and we wonder *why*. Why does the relationship have to end? Why did the love one die? Why does health have to fail? Why do illnesses have to rule? Why were we betrayed? Why were we rejected? Why is life so unfair? *Why, why, why?*

Jesus had lived as best he could. He had loved all. He had accepted all persons, even those rejected by others. He had done the right thing. He had been honest. He had communed with his God. He had lived a righteous life. He had reached out to those who were hurting.

And then on this day long ago, Jesus entered the very gates of hell and despair on a hill called Golgotha. He was there on this day long ago. And more intense than the spikes in his wrist and ankles or the thorns on his head were the piercing questions of *why, why*? And especially the mother of all questions, "My God, My God, why have you forsaken me?" If we do not deny it, it is the question of our soul at times as well. Thank God this is not the end. Thank God there is more to come. Amen.

17

Easter: Your Passion Can Live Again!

Preparatory Reading: Mark 14:50

> Where is your passion in life? Well, you say, "I once had passion. At one time I was a passionate person—I felt alive." Is your passion for life in the past? Was your passion for life somehow buried long ago? Could this be the Easter when you find your passion is resurrected? Think about it. Welcome to a time of meditation and reflection.

Prayer: Oh, God, sometimes we just get lost or we lose our way. We can also lose our passion and be just putting one foot in front of the other but not really moving with energy and life. May we find our life in you again this day. Amen.

At the end of his life, Jesus did not appear successful. The scriptures state in the earliest gospel, in Mark 14:50, "Then everyone deserted him and fled." Now, how would you like to come to the end of your life and it be said of all your friends, "They all forsook him or her and fled." How would you like that for an epitaph on your tombstone, "They all deserted *him* and fled" or "They all deserted *her* and fled"?

It did not appear that Jesus accomplished much at the time of his death. Even his closest disciples tucked their tails and ran. And one of the leaders by the name of Peter denied that he even knew him—not one time, not two times, but three times.

Jesus died the death of a common criminal. He died with no status, except as another of the many rebels who died by crucifixion. He didn't even live very long, dying in his early thirties. And he did not actually have much of a following when he died or for the first century or so after his death. The very early church was a struggling and fledging little disjointed band of persons. Jesus did not appear to have accomplished much with his life.

There was a short life—a criminal's death on a cross, abandonment by his followers, not much to impress, not much to get excited about. Would you get on board with such a miserable failure? Would you choose to join up with such a pitiful record of success? Would you risk your life to follow this person named Jesus?

What happened to the teachings of this unsuccessful—at least by most standards—teacher named Jesus? How is it that his teachings are now taught around the globe? How is it that those who fled him later died for him? How is it that they developed a passion for him that motivated them to the ends of the earth?

Thomas Connelan wrote, "One person with passion is better than forty who are merely interested."[28] You see, it doesn't take too many passionate people to change the world. It doesn't take too many who are passionate and genuine with their beliefs to effect change.

At first, the disciples were devastated. They could not bear to deal with the death of Jesus. But as they pulled themselves together, they realize that nothing could stop the power of what they had experienced in Jesus.

When someone meets your spiritual longings, can you forget them? When someone values you like you are the only person in the world, can you resist the force of his or her influence? When someone loves you into new life, can you forget that person? The disciples realized that in Jesus, they had seen and experienced God as they had never before experienced God. No tomb can stop the power of one who has transformed you into "a new being," to use an expression of theologian Paul Tillich.

Reflect with me for a moment on just a little of what the disciples had witnessed with Jesus. He was a lover of the little children. He valued them and affirmed their worth. Jesus was a liberator of those who were oppressed by society, by sin, and by disease. They had seen Jesus free persons from their pain, like the woman who touched the helm of his garment. He knew the touch of faith, and it got his attention. He knew when there was a special need, even when he was in a crowd and he was on a mission. He did not get distracted from the hurt and pain of individuals. Do you hurt in some way this morning? Jesus is deeply concerned about you.

The disciples witnessed him stand his ground with the demoniacs, the crazy persons of the tombs—the men of whom all were afraid, ones who had broken the chains that held them, ones who roamed among the cemetery with no hope of change. No one saw any positive possibilities in such persons, except for Jesus. Jesus saw them as worthwhile, and soon he had them sitting at his feet in their right minds. Do you feel you have no worth this morning? Jesus sees you as precious and of infinite value.

The disciples had witnessed the absolute integrity of Jesus. He made no compromises when principle was at stake, even when it meant he would be harmed. He did not seek conflict for no reason, but he never flinched when right came up against might. He believed in truth and followed truth wherever it took him. Do you need to do battle with bad habits or the powers of darkness? Jesus is ready to fight beside you.

Then there was the compassion of Jesus. He wept unashamedly over the people of Jerusalem for whom he felt so deeply. He had some sense of the impending crisis in Jerusalem and how the city will be destroyed. Jesus was a person of great compassion, a feeling deep within that even groans and aches for others in pain. Do you think no one knows your desperate soul search for someone who cares for you? Jesus knows your longing and wants you to experience his love.

And they heard his teaching and now they reviewed his teachings over and over like a tape in their heads. He taught the story of the father with two sons and the sons rebelled, one by leaving home and one by rebelling at home. Jesus even drove home the point about the father who ran to his son who was lost and hugged and kissed him repeatedly. And Jesus said, "This is what your heavenly Father is like. He is like a father who forgives and loves his children." Have you been rebelling against God and everyone else? Jesus wants to welcome you home!

It powerfully came back to the disciples in their sorrow of how Jesus also taught about God as the good shepherd who leaves the ninety-nine and goes out and risks all to save the one lost sheep. And Jesus said, "This is also what your heavenly father is like. And when he finds you, he gently places you over his shoulder and carries you back home and nurtures you." Jesus wants to take you in his arms and remove you from the danger of wanderings and put oil on your wounds and comfort you.

The disciples remembered other examples of the impact of Jesus upon persons. Like his impact upon the funny little man by the name of Zacchaeus—a short man who climbed up into a sycamore tree so he could catch a glimpse of Jesus, a man who was hard as nails on the outside and despised for his ruthless cheating as a publican with his oppression of the poor—Jesus saw something worthwhile even in Zacchaeus, and he told him to get down out of the tree and Jesus went home with him and Zacchaeus became a new being that day. Do you need to have someone look beneath the false exterior of your life and find the good in you? That is exactly what Jesus does.

And there was the woman caught in the act of adultery. It appeared that she was framed or trapped by some of the religious folk, and they were ready to stone her. However, Jesus did not pick up a stone; instead, he picked up her crashed heart and she became

COMING BACK TO FAITH

a new being that very day. Jesus can begin making you into a new person even today.

In the final events of his life, he was treated as a criminal, but he died with dignity like a God. He did not recant. He did not cower away. He did not compromise to save his own neck. He served the disciples in the upper room when they should have been serving and comforting him. He loved them to the last. He even prayed for the forgiveness of those who drove the spikes into his hands. Even on the cross, he looked down upon them with his eyes of unstoppable love. And his eyes of unstoppable love are looking upon you this day.

Now let me go back say it again. At the end of his life, Jesus he did not appear successful. As we have seen, the scriptures state, in the earliest gospel in Mark 14:50, "They all deserted him and fled." And let me ask you a question, How is it that this unsuccessful person is now worshipped by millions?

Even the few events and teaching of his life that we just reflected upon reveal to us that the power of this person by the name of Jesus is not going to remain in the tomb! There is no tomb strong enough to hold his kind of power! There is no grave to contain the influence of such a person as Jesus!

Jesus shattered our definitions of success. Jesus burst our expectation of what it means to accomplish much in life. Jesus turned our world upside down and inside out. Doesn't his unlimited grace and his limitless love astound you? It should, and it should awaken a sleeping passion deep inside you.

And let me ask you this: Where is the spirit of Christ to live today? Where is his power to be manifest today? It is an astonishing fact; it should find a place to live in you and me. Remember that quote I used earlier: "One person with passion is better than forty who are merely interested."

Are we going to have the passion about Jesus that the disciples found after their great disappointment as they reviewed their experience with him? Are you passionate about Jesus and his teachings and way of life? Jesus wants one person with passion today, this moment; it only takes one to make an impact.

Do you have passion about Jesus or just a mere interest? Could it be that this will be the Easter that you will point back to and say, "On that day, I went from merely being interested in Jesus to finding the passion of Jesus in my life"? Passion can free you from your tomb this morning!

- Come out of that old tomb where you have died and find your life again!
- Come out of that old tomb where you have died and find your dream again!
- Come out of that old tomb where you have died and find your hope again!
- Come out of that old tomb where you have died and begin to live again!

Lost hope? Lost life? Lost passion? Lost purpose? There is no better place than on Easter Sunday to begin living again. Your life can be resurrected from whatever tomb that is seeking to contain it this morning.

Life does not have to go on as before. No tomb can contain the life and spirit-giving force found in Jesus. Come forth, come forth from the tombs that so restrict and so hamper and so limit and so frustrate and so destroy your life. Come forth into the life-giving way of Jesus this very day. Jesus desires to be resurrected in you today, right now, at this very moment, in your history. Amen.

18

Easter Weeping May Linger for a Night, but Joy Returns!

Preparatory Reading: John 20:1–18; Psalm 30:5b

How do we live life with all its difficulties? How do we find hope in the dark corners of life? When the darkness overwhelms us, what do we do? Sometimes we, too, find ourselves encased in a dark tomb from which there appears no escape, no relief.

Can we find any way to roll the stone of despair away? The Good News shouts, "Yes you can!" Think about it. Welcome to a time of reflection and meditation.

Prayer: Oh, God, we have been struggling. This week, we have ridden the up-and-down, emotional roller coaster of holy week. May we find that, in spite of all the obstacles that life throws at us, there is ultimate stability in living with you and following your way this day. We pray this in the spirit of the one who turns tombs into wombs of new birth. Amen.

"Weeping may linger for the night but joy comes with the morning," Psalm 30:5b says.[29] What a wonderful text this is! What a text to have in your memory and one I really want to put in your subconscious for you to recall when needed.

On Friday, we did our weeping, and we rode the emotional roller coaster of Holy Week down into the depths of despair and the belly of hell. We drank the dregs of bitterness. We realized, at least to some degree, the utter disillusionment and shattered hope of the follows of Jesus when they saw him from a distance hanging on a criminal's cross. The one who had been their hope was nailed to a cross, and his life snuffed out. The one who had opened up for them the way to the heart of God had a sword open up his side. The one who had been their king was mocked and ridiculed and hurt by a cruel crown of thorns being shoved down on his head. He who had exhibited the greatest tenderness toward all persons, even those despised by others, was treated with the greatest cruelty. All hope was lost. Intense darkness covered their souls.

There was nothing to hang on to; his disciples were free-falling into an abyss of horrific emotions. Weeping did not bring relief. Sobbing did not help. And they too soon cried out to God as Christ did on the cross, "My God, My God why have you forsaken me?" Even God could not bring comfort. And it is the cry of the ages, when life is so hard it breaks us.

You and I have cried this phrase at times, if we have lived very long at all, "My God, My God why have you forsaken me?" (Matt. 27:46). We too have experienced abandonment, rejection, relationship crisis, and loneliness in some form. Jesus on the cross and his disciples on that Friday long ago were a microcosm of suffering humanity and the *why* questions of life that shred our souls into tiny pieces. *Why is life so unfair? Why do the innocent suffer? Why do we suffer?* All the questions are summed up in the one from Psalms that Jesus cried from the cross: "My God, My God why have you forsaken me?" (Ps. 22:1).

However—and it is the most powerful of words—"weeping may linger for a night but joy comes with the morning!" Easter shouts to us, "The night is not the end, the darkness of life will not last forever!" Can you hear the shout of Easter this morning? Let it resonate, let it continue bouncing around in your soul and bring you hope!

The bad in life comes, but then life can change and good things can happen. The difficulty may not endure. The end may become the beginning. We must hold on to these concepts to live fully. Things do often get better. The bad thing can transform and be the beginning of something new. That is it! I love the symbols and rituals and metaphors of Christianity because they are so real to life, and they help us in life. They relate to where the rubber meets the road. "Weeping may endure for a night, but joy comes in the morning!" Oh, what a hope and comfort is in these words!

William Sloane Coffin said, "It is a Good Friday world."[30] In many ways, at some times, the world is one of despair, but may I suggest to you that for the followers of Jesus, we can shout instead "It is an Easter world"? A world filled with hope and joy. Yes, there is weeping, but the joy comes to overtake the weeping. Light comes into the places of darkness and dispels them. Love overcomes the dark nights of the soul and moves us to joy.

One of the followers of Jesus, Mary, was walking in her darkness. Yet it was more than the darkness of night; it was the darkness of a soul at great unrest. She was walking into the darkness, and that is what we have to do at such times. It states that early that Easter morning, "while it was still dark" (John 20:1). You see, she walked into the darkness, and we must do so as well. We must walk in and face the darkness, if we are to overcome it.

We cannot flee from it, we cannot hide from it. Let me challenge you to walk into your darkness for there, discoveries will be made. Oh, we may have to cry out with Mary, "They have taken the Lord out of the tomb, and we don't know where they have put him" (John 20:2b). I had never noticed it previously, but as I was reading her words this time, I realized how much anguish there were in her words, like the anguish in the words of Jesus on the cross, "My God, My God why have you forsaken me?" Again, these are the cries of humanity in pain.

The tomb becomes the womb of a new experience, and it gives birth to joy unspeakable. Remember it states, "While it was yet dark," and while it was yet dark, while she was in the darkness, Jesus was waiting for her and spoke to her as she wept. Jesus is waiting for us as well outside the tomb of our own darkness. If we will keep walking in the darkness and not give up, we will discover Jesus waiting for us in the darkness.

However, it is often only as day breaks, only at the last hour, that we find him. "Weeping may linger for the night [*and it certainly seems like it endures all night long!*], but joy comes with the morning." Hang on! Don't give up! Joy comes in the morning!

We have all said it to someone and maybe it was not so helpful at the time—words like "I know this is difficult for you, but I know some good will come out of it and you will be stronger as a result." It may be inappropriate to say, but we all know, as we look back on our own lives if we have lived very long, that it is generally true. However, when we are overwhelmed and in the darkness, we cannot see and we need a good friend to hold our hand.

There is something in Easter that overwhelms us because it truly calls us to a new and transformed life. And even as bad as the darkness is, sometimes, it is so familiar that we are afraid to venture into the new life God wants to give us.

When plunged into the darkness, we sometimes have an inkling that life has somehow drastically changed in some manner; and as we are trying to find our way, we are also fearing the unknown. There is a part of our lives that grieves the loss of whatever was before. Even if something new is dawning in our lives, we are afraid.

My friends, are you ready to move out of the darkness, out of the weeping, and into the joy of Easter? It is not just all an emotional high; it is a change of life. It is transformational if we truly experience it. Once we really encounter this one called Christ who was willing to die for what he stood for and for whom he loved, we cannot be the same. The past is crucified, and the way it was and the way we were can no longer be the same.

Weeping may endure for a night or even for a lifetime, but when we truly encounter Jesus Christ and his way, joy comes and brings a fresh morning into our lives!

What a wonderful time to step out of the darkness and into the light! What a fantastic time is Easter to seek to allow our lives to be resurrected from the tomb of despair! What a tremendous opportunity to move into the newness of life that Christ provides!

Yes, weeping may endure for a night or even longer, but joy comes in the morning as we encounter the Christ who dispels darkness and brings light and life to our souls. Happy Easter to you! Amen.

THE PENTECOST

The Pentecost experience is pretty wild in the scriptures, but I think it is descriptive of great change and transformation taking place. There are times in life when we need extraordinary experiences to awaken us.

Pentecost

19

The Spirit at Work

Preparatory Reading: Acts 2:1–21

What is your approach to persons who differ from you? What is your approach to persons who believe differently than your do? When someone presents an opinion that is contrary to the way you believe, do you feel threatened? Do you start to defend your belief? Do you listen to what they have to say? Do we have anything to learn from others or do we have all truth? Think about it. Welcome to a time of meditation and reflection.

Prayer: Oh, God, we have so often failed to allow your spirit to be our spirit. Instead, we have maintained the spirit of fear and insecurity. May we come to rest more in you and know that we have nothing to fear when you are in us and we are in you. In the spirit of Jesus who built bridges and crossed barriers to minister to all persons, we pray. Amen.

William Willimon, the former chaplain at Duke University Chapel, once mentioned that

Someone has said the church is somewhat like a football huddle, the huddle that players go into at a football game. You know that something important is being said there, but you can't understand a word of it, and all you can see is their rear-ends.[31]

Many persons have no idea, especially today, about what is happening in the church. We can no longer assume that persons coming to visit the church have heard the great stories of the Hebrew and Christian scriptures. Many people wonder what in the world we are doing in church these days. What is church all about? What is the church doing? Where is the church headed? And I suppose we should go ahead and admit that some of us in the church wonder the same things at times!

Church life can be very confusing at times, even from the inside. But imagine what it is like for many today those who have never been a part of it to look at the church. It must be terribly confusing. There are many denominations, many differences, and many theologies. It is like various Christians speak different languages, and of course, we have Christians who literally speak in many different languages. But even those who speak the same language speak in different ways and have different beliefs. Imagine a person who never went to church awakes one morning and decides to go to a Catholic church one Sunday and then, since they are exploring churches, decide to go to a holiness service the next Sunday. It could be rather confusing.

And when comparing the church to a football huddle and persons only seeing the backside, we certainly know that the church tends to often show its backside, if you please. In the past, I have written and spoken about the sick side of the church from time to time and how sick persons can use religion in very sick ways. However, on the other hand, I have written and spoken often on the positive aspects of the church.

Listen to these words I wrote a few years ago:

> The church should mirror Christ, but it too often fails at the task. To many people the church is simply bricks and mortar devoid of the spirit of Christ. Yet the

weak attempts by the church in its better moments to manifest Christ are what keep others in the church. We have no other place to go that offers so much potential even in the midst of human blunderings and failings.[32]

May I suggest to you this morning that the better moments of the church are when is it allowing God's spirit to empower it and transform it. Today is Pentecost Sunday, the day we recognize as the birthday of the church. Luke, in the Acts of the Apostles, has a profound story that crystallizes the coming of the spirit at Pentecost. The author of the gospel of John seems to have the spirit come on Easter, but Luke puts the emphasis upon the experience at Pentecost. And, of course, the writer is finding new meanings for the Jewish holy days and transforming them into Christian holy days so this added to his ability to do that.

In our scripture for today, we find the disciples being filled with the spirit—in other words, being empowered by the spirit of God. May I suggest that when we think about or experience being filled with the spirit, this is what it is all about: we are empowered by the spirit of God. Paul Tillich, the great theologian, wrote that Spirit is another word for "God Present."[33] Just as Jesus is our prime example of one empowered by the spirit of God, God was present in Jesus.

Perhaps even when the church is empowered by the spirit of God, persons looking on may still be confused for a while. Note in our passage that onlookers thought at first that the disciples had too much wine. Of course, it begs the question I must ask, Would anyone looking on us think that we have had too much wine? We are rarely euphoric—or, in other words, extremely happy—in the church. Maybe we are so contained and proper that we look more like we are drugged with an antispontaneity pill than we are drunk with too much wine. I don't know.

The whole story we read from our scripture is designed by Luke to be a reversal of the Tower of Babel story from Genesis 11. Remember the story of humans all having the same language and attempting to build a tower to the heavens and it was seen as arrogant by God so that God confused the languages so humans could not communicate and the building of the tower had to stop. It is a great story or allegory of how we are confused and have maybe forgotten the language of God and how we rarely understand each other or God.

In our story for today in Acts 2, there is an understanding that returns to humans who are empowered by God. In this scripture, we have the Tower of Babel reversed. At Babel, humankind became fragmented and conflicted and confused as evidenced by the differences of language. At Pentecost, the believers spoke different languages but became united by the spirit.

Scholar Marcus Borg was my reference on this, and he points out that the Pentecost was the restoration of the commonality of humanity that occurred at the breakdown of Babel. It is a summary of a gradual beginning of the early church that is found in our present passage in Acts 2.[34]

Pentecost reveals how God would like to reverse Babel. Pentecost calls for unity rather than division. Pentecost moves toward understanding rather than confusion. The spirit of God is one of unity and communication and dialogue and the divisive movements of evil and hateful humanity where we put each other down and attack each other are challenged and dispelled.

However, we know that the church somehow often shows its backside and we know that our differences are not always in fact burned away. But note for us the key is that when the church is filled with the spirit—or, in other words, empowered—by God, there is a commonality that we find in true humanity an acceptance of one another.

Karen Armstrong who writes on the history of Christianity also wrote these words: "It's time we moved beyond toleration into appreciation of the other's faith and culture."[35] There are churches that officially celebrate what is called Pluralism Sunday. Pluralism is a celebration of the value of all healthy religions. Maybe part of what the tower of Babel symbolisms is our division among each other and the untold harm that has come down through the centuries from condemning and fighting and even, at times, killing all those who differ from us.

This grand conflict between religions where one is pitted against another rather than seeking commonalities among them has caused untold destruction in its pathway. It has led to exclusivism, ostracism, and prejudice, as well as hatred. It has turned many from any religious interest at all. Pentecost calls us to be more inclusive, which means that we seek to reach out a hand to each other. It says, "I can learn and grow from our relationship even when we are of differing religions and your religion can be valued by me." We should tolerate each other's religions and find ways to cooperate and communicate. Pluralism seeks to value the good in all healthy religions and promotes that there are multiple ways that can lead us to understanding of spiritual realities.

I do not know where you fall in your thinking about other belief systems, but I hope you, at least, will ponder what you think in this regard. Pluralism does not mean we cannot disagree and debate, but it brings a different attitude to our interactions, I believe. My tradition is the way of Jesus, but I do believe I can learn from the religious traditions of others. And I do not believe we have to be threatened by them.

Maybe part of what Pentecost should teach us is that when we are spirit filled, we will seek to find commonality and bridges toward dialogue. Maybe part of the way that the spirit of God is truly evident in our lives is that we get to the point of where we are secure enough in our own faith that we can be open to true listening and dialogue with others. When you look at Jesus, he was involved in discussions with those of different faiths.

Maybe there is a destructive part of our religion that sets up walls with different faiths and religions. Are we unwilling to learn from them? I hope not. The confusion of Babel continues to exist if we build walls, and as we do so, we continue to miss the coming together of Pentecost. Maybe part of the spirit of God working in our lives is embracing all peoples as we say we believe that God does.

Perhaps, I am suggesting to you today, we have failed to realize the power of Pentecost, the power of God's spirit, because we are erecting our own walls, our own towers of Babel; therefore, the confusion and broken communication of Babel continues in our midst.

However, I am suggesting that an indication of God's spirit moving upon us will be our appreciation of the differences among us both within the church, outside of the church, and even among various belief systems. When this occurs, Pentecost will have fully come into our midst. Could we tolerate it? Could we embrace it? Amen.

POST-EASTER ORDINARY DAYS

The ordinary days are times during the year when there is not a special Christian day or season. Who among us has never had a ho-hum day? Who among us has not had difficulty at times with the sameness of life? There is something about ordinary days that is comforting with their routines and habits that give us some continuity. However, on some ordinary days, our passion of life may ebb and flow. We may get stuck or we may long for better days.

Post-Easter Ordinary Time

20

Stumbling and Falling but on the Road with Jesus Again![36]

Preparatory Reading: Luke 24:13–35

> I wonder how often God is seeking to be more than a passing stranger in our lives and yet we recognize it not? I wonder how often God goes unnoticed in our lives because we have so much pulling at our attention? So many distractions that cause us to lose our passion, lose our life energy, and that cause us to stumble and fall and become discouraged and disappointed.
>
> Where is God as we are making such a journey? Think about it. Welcome to a time of meditation and reflection.

Prayer: Oh, Lord, our eyes so often are covered with spiritual cataracts that blur and confuse and distort our view of you, and we stumble. Somehow, we do not see your presence with us or we do not bring you into focus or we see you as a stranger. We pray that you would bring healing to our sight that we might see Jesus this morning and find our passion once again. Amen.

We mentioned how Palm Sunday could be a parade to nowhere if we stopped there. We then wrote of the fact that we were getting somewhere—and somewhere special indeed—on Easter Sunday. We have looked at our stumbling and falling in the journey of life and the marvelous grace of our God.

Today, we will look at a road that begins as a road to nowhere but ends up being a road of such great joy unspeakable even though the disciples are stumbling and falling in the darkness. However, this is a different kind of stumbling and falling because now they know they are on the road with Jesus once again. You do know the difference, do you not?

Stumbling and falling, because you are depressed and have your head down is very different from stumbling and falling in joy and happiness. The baseball player who stumbles and falls running the bases has a very different experience from the one who jumps up with his teammates and falls down after winning the game.

It was like an echo from a deep, dark well that kept whispering "There is no hope, there is no hope." The echo alternated with a rolling thundercloud that kept roaring out "Life is just a big disappointment." A jagged bolt of emotional lightning pierced their hearts like a knife, and the pain struck again and again. This kind of lighting could strike in the same heart much more than once.

Their hopes, their hopes had been shattered like a window being pierced by a rock. They had plunged to the deep valley so low—and this was no roller coaster, there was no raising again to the heights. It would never be the same again. Jesus was dead.

They were walking in the shadow of a cross, a cross upon which they saw their Messiah die. They had witnessed the awful scenes Jesus had experienced. They had witnessed his death as a common criminal. They had lost their Lord, and having lost him, they had lost all hope.

The scripture states that they "had hoped" (Luke 24:20). *Hope* in the past tense is a tragedy. When you add the past tense to *hope*, it is like adding a coffin on a wagon like they add to the beautiful horse that pulls the coffin of great person when they die. When you add the past tense to *hope*, it is like a person calling code blue at the hospital when someone is breathing their last breath.

You just cannot add the past tense to *hope* without making life very complicated. You cannot add the past tense to *hope* without adding a deadly weight to a life and causing it to sink like the *Titanic*. Hope faded into the past is like the dreary night sky after the brilliant fireworks have dissipated in nothingness. *Hope* in the past tense destroys our passion. *Hope that is past is really no hope at all.*

Sometimes people attempt to live on past hopes, but it is a retched existence. It offers little sustenance to the soul. It keeps them frozen in times long ago, never to find the opportunities of the present or the future.

How you ever lived on past hope? Do you ever attempt to get by on past hopes? Past hopes are only crumbs of existence. As we live longer, some dreams may die, but what about when hope dies as well?

And churches can sometimes attempt to live on past hopes. Churches can be paralyzed by adding the past tense to *hope*—we had *hoped* to be a great church, we had *hoped* to grow, we had *hoped* to minister in this community, we had *hoped* to continue with our passion—we had, we had, we had. Adding the past tense to *hope* is a tragedy indeed, isn't it?

At first, they had attempted to find comfort and solace in the company of their fellow believers, but now it was time to return home and begin the week's work. Life somehow has to go on amid life's disappointments. So slowly—for depressed persons walk slowly—they begin their seven-mile journey back to the village of Emmaus. The sun was sinking lower in the sky, but the feelings of these two disciples are sinking lower still. Darkness was soon to fall upon the earth, but they were experiencing a darkness heavier than sunset.

Drained from the emotional disappointment and exhaustion, their feet dragged along in the dry dust. One of them kicks a stick along in the dust as he walks, anything to habitually break the monotony of their forever walk. In their pain, they sought to find comfort in talking with each other. At times their, lips quivered with bereavement.

Why in the world do we have another story of such sadness in the gospel of Luke? Isn't it time to get over it and move on to more positive things? I mean, Luke, you have just about finished your gospel story; and here at the end, you waste valuable space telling about depressed disciples? We know you also wrote Acts, but do you think we will want to read Acts when you are ending this gospel on such a downer? It isn't much of a way to get us to anticipate a sequel.

Well, I don't know exactly why Luke included this story, but it is written in such a way as to be relevant to people down through the centuries. Who has not found disappointment at some point in life? Who has lived very long and not had their life shattered at some point with profound grief? Who has never attempted to live on the bland diet of past experiences? Who has been so stuck in one way of thinking as to be blinded to opportunities all around them? Who has not missed the presence of God all around us and lived as though God were absent or even dead?

These are the roads most traveled by humanity. Most walk such dusty roads for much of their lives—eyes drooping, kicking sticks, limited focus. Some remain on such roads all their days.

Are you walking on a road to Emmaus this morning—head downcast, face to the ground? It is a road most often traveled, and it is a painful one. Maybe you have been on a road to Emmaus for oh too long. Maybe you have seen it as your lot in life. *This is my fate, this is my destination in life, this is my lot in life*, you once thought. *I continue on this journey that detaches me from the present and any hope of the future. God appears to be missing from this road.*

Maybe this story reveals to us the utter failure of our lives when we are blind to the spiritual parts of life that are all around us. Jesus, in the story, is walking with the disciples; but they do not recognize him. The most profound spiritual experience that they had known in the past was being with Jesus, but now their emotional and spiritual state keeps them from the very person that can offer to lead them to greater spiritual experiences.

These disciples are on the road to Emmaus. Maybe many of us are on the road to Emmaus and are blinded to the search for meaning and purpose and spiritual realities, even those right beside us. We are taking the road most traveled, and it is a hell of a road and a road to hell.

The road to Emmaus is the ordinary road of humankind. It is the road traveled by most. We travel it blinded, oblivious, or ignoring, running from, or denying the purpose that God wants to give us in life. We have often lost our way and we go deeper and deeper into the abyss. We fall further and further into existential nothingness, and we are afraid.

But my friends, Jesus can come up beside us to set us on course. Jesus can be a transformational force within us to turn the road to Emmaus into a highway of adventure and challenge and salvation. Jesus can be the one to open our eyes to live life to the fullest and find depth and meaning and purpose. Jesus can restore us to grace and peace and of hope in the present tense! Jesus can give us hope burning within, hope that is alive!

Notice what is says in Luke 24:32: "Were not our hearts burning within us while he talked with us on the road." You see, when Jesus walks and talks with us on the road of life, the journey becomes an adventure; and our hearts begin to burn with passion for living a life worth living.

Have you lost your passion for life this morning? Are you wandering on the road to Emmaus—face downcast, starved from living on past hopes, feeling like nothing matters anymore? Are you just kicking a stick along life's journey to break the monotony?

If so, please allow me to make a suggestion. Pause along enough to allow God's spirit to open your eyes to all the spiritual reality around you. Allow Jesus to be your hero within that calls you forth to a new life of adventure that is filled with passion for living and serving.

Don't just stumble along on the road most traveled. Don't just kick the stick on the way to Emmaus. Allow Jesus to transform your journey so that you are running and jumping stumbling and falling in a different manner because it is with a joy that cannot be contained and you need to share it with someone, anyone! It can burn within your soul as a passion that will not stop. Amen.

21

We Will Not Be Ordinary Christians Called to Love as Christ Loved!

Preparatory Reading: 1 John 4:7–21

How do you sum up what you believe? If it takes you more than a few seconds you have probably already lost the attention of anyone in our nanosecond society. But how would you succinctly describe your faith? Think about it. Welcome to a time of meditation and reflection.

Prayer: Oh, God, here we go again making life and Christianity so complicated. And yet maybe the love that some of us took in with our mother's milk is closer to the reality of what matters than all our high-sounding theologies. May we find the simplicity of the gospel today is our prayer in the name of the one who walked this earth and loved simply and profoundly. Amen.

I want you to know that I have a very scientific and elaborate and organized manner of choosing my sermon titles. For example, this meditation came from a sermon that went this way:

I had been reviewing the text and thinking and reading about the lectionary passage in 1 John that I would speak upon. It then came time in the middle of the week and I had to send in the bulletin material. I came up with the last part of the sermon title based upon my reflection of the passage—"The Call to Love as Christ Loved!"—which seemed to me to be a strong imperative from the passage. But I felt that I needed a phase at the beginning of the title.

As I was pondering this, I looked at the notes that I had jotted down from the leadership team meeting I had just attended because I was also thinking of any announcements we needed for the bulletin as well. And as I looked at my notes in my own handwriting, which has been compared to chicken scratching, I saw a phrase that was just what I wanted for my sermon title, and it read, "We Will Not Be Ordinary Christians." Now that fit well for the sermon title: "We Will Not Be Ordinary Christians: Called to Love as Christ Loved." It sounded pretty good.

However, as I looked more closely at the phrase from my notes from the leadership meeting, I realized that my writing did not say "We will not be ordinary Christians" but "We will not be ordering chicken," and it was what I had written about the fact that we would not be ordering chicken for our Wednesday potluck! This lets you in on how elaborate and methodical my sermon title process is!

Perhaps, if you do not think I am absolutely crazy, you see how my mind—maybe my subconscious—or maybe the even the spirit speaking to my mind, in some fashion, made it so that I read "We will not be ordering chicken" as "We will not be ordinary Christians"!

Do you recall that wonderful story written by the great theologian Karl Barth? The parable has various versions, but it goes like this: people in a village were awakened by the beautiful music coming for the bell tower of the church. And they thought, *Oh, isn't that such beautiful music?* But what they didn't know was that the minister had been climbing the stairway of the bell tower and had lost his footing and, on his way down from falling, grabbed the rope to the church bell and was there dangling in the bell tower at the end of the rope, trying to hang on for dear life.[37]

Perhaps all of this points to the folly of preaching. Those of us who stand in this holy spot are mere mortals with our own sins, mistakes, and shortcomings; and often we are dangling at the very edge of life, barely hanging on ourselves. But the miracle is that somehow, sometimes, God's spirit speaks through all our humanness to encourage a soul. That is the folly and the greatness of preaching.

"We will not be ordinary Christians"—wow! How I like that! How I wish we would believe that. Not in any sense of thinking, we are better than other Christians, not in the sense that we think we are more spiritual or have some special insight. But what if we decided that we would not be ordinary Christians in the way we loved? What if we decided that by the power of God, we would love as Christ loved? Would it make a difference? You bet it would!

The passage we have for today is a wonderful summary of the basics of what it means to be a Christian. In fact, the entire gospel is summed up here. If you had to put the entire gospel into three words, if you had to put the good news of God in a nutshell, or in one short sentence, what would you write or say?

Well, here it is in this passage: look at the end of 1 John 4:8: "God is love." That is it, is it not? You can come up with all kinds of elaborate ways of defining and describing Christianity and God, but none do justice until you simplify it to this. None are so simple yet as profound as this. None tell us our value as much as this. And none tell us what should be our calling as much as these three words: God is love.

Now, remember the early churches were struggling and were having people split off and leave and there was false teaching confusing many of the faithful. And note that at the beginning of this chapter, the author notes in 1 John 4:1 that the spirits should be tested. So, the context even for this passage on love is to combat false teaching and false spirits. And what better way to promote the truths of Christianity than to bring the focus to the foundational cornerstone of love!

Love is the foundational stone for a healthy and happy Christian life as well. What we believe is this: Love originates with our God. The text says this as well (1 John 4:7–8). The source of all love is God. God is not the source of anger, criticism, or condemnation as some make God to be. No. God is the source of love, and love flows from God. Unless you picture God as someone who knows you completely (with all your sins and failures) and yet loves you completely, you have not seen God.

If you imagine a judgmental, stern face looking at you when you think of God, you have transferred some faulty, earthly image to God and you are badly mistaken and will be profoundly unhappy. God is love, and any image we have of God must be an image of one who loves us with unlimited, prodigal, and extravagant love. It is God's nature to love you and me. God is love—that is the gospel in summary!

Notice the kind of negative parallelism found in verse 8: "Whoever does not love does not know God." This is stating in the negative what is found in verse 7: "Everyone who loves has been born of God and knows God."

Apparently, some of the false teachers were claiming that there was some other source for love and were treating others badly; they were certainly not showing love toward them. So the author states clearly that the initiative for love originates with God. You see my friends, God is seeking us. God takes the initiative. God is the hound of heaven coming to find us, longing for relationship with us. That is the God of love.

And the author states that God's love was manifest in Jesus. Jesus revealed to us most clearly what the love of God is like. He went about doing good to all. Houston Smith, in his book, *The Soul of Christianity*, writes these wonderful words: "The Gospels vibrate with wonder at Jesus' actions."[38] And that wonder is the way that Jesus conceptualized and revealed God as a God of infinite love. And Jesus revealed that love is not just some mystical theory or distant abstraction; he went about loving people and showing them the love of God with his actions and his caring. He revealed that love is relationship and without relationship love has no power.

The author of 1 John reasons from the origins of love in God to the reason that Christians should love. This is our inspiration to love, this is our motivation to love, this is our ability to love—God first loved us. We respond to others with love because love has impacted our own lives. God loves us completely in spite of our failure and we are to love real people with real problems and unlovely features.

Note, the height of righteousness, the pinnacle of success, the mark of the Christian is that we allow God's love to be manifest to others through us! We are so loved that we should have love for others. This is not to earn God's or other people's favor; it is not motivated by fear for as the author states in 1 John 4:18, there is "no fear in love." We love because it becomes our nature to love as God works within us. And by the way, you can test some of the current spirits that abound by how much fear they seek to generate. Love casts out fear; false teachings promote fear.

God is stating very clearly and simply that love comes from God and that the greatest calling upon us is to be a people of love in action. Just as the "the Gospels vibrate with wonder at Jesus," as Houston Smith put it and we quoted above, the church and our communities should vibrate with the wonder of Christians who go about loving the unlovable.

The call to us today is to be loving. It is simple yet profound, and it only will happen as we know the love of God in our own experience.

It may be true that my church or your church will not be ordering chicken for the potluck on Wednesday. But I hope it is also true that we will not be ordinary Christians in our love. May our love not be a potluck of various forms and counterfeits of love, but may we serve real love of God in our churches and in our places in the world. May our love break all the confinements and conditions we put upon it, and may we begin to love with the love of God in Christ. Amen.

22

When the Groans and Moans of Life Are Too Great to Bear

Preparatory Reading: Romans 8:22–27

Do you ever get confused by life and not know which way to turn or who to go to for help? Does it sometimes seem that all you can do is gurgle some ungodly sounds from somewhere deep in your soul and you don't want anyone to hear such awful noises and you certainly don't expect anyone, even God to understand. Well, think again, for God hears our deepest hurts. God is always listening. Think about it. Welcome to a time of meditation and reflection.

Prayer: Oh, God, there are times when we have unspeakable sorrow and hurt and no one understands or seems to even care. May we somehow find the light of your love shining in the midst of the dark moments of life. We pray in the name of the one who was the life and the light of all, Jesus Christ. Amen.

Life just doesn't always go as it should. Have you ever gone to the store and somehow ended up with one of those buggies or shopping carts that has a bad wheel? So, you push it along, and it squeals your presence to everyone; and every time you turn a corner, you can imagine someone saying, "Oh no, there comes squeaky!" Or sometimes they have a wheel that thumps. I got one at Home Depot just this week. And every time the wheel went around, it went *thump*. 90 percent of the wheel was OK, but then there was the thump so there I went—*thump, thump, thump, thump.*

Isn't that illustrative of life itself? A lot of life can go well, but then there are the thumps. Sometimes I want to say to God "God, just stop giving me real-life illustrations for writing, I can find some somewhere else." But life happens to ministers as well, and maybe God gives me extra experiences for meditation illustrations, I don't know.

Life does not always go as it should. Sometimes, we get interrupted in the daily grind. During the ordinary days of life and living, which can be difficult enough at times, we have bumps and thumps along the way that disturb us. Charles Smith wrote about this. According to him, you know your day is not going well when

- your income tax check bounces;
- your birthday cake collapses from the weight of the candles;
- you wake up and discover your waterbed broke and then realize that you don't have a water bed;
- your twin brother or sister forgets your birthday; or
- the bird singing outside your window is a buzzard.[39]

Life doesn't always go as it should. We have the saying as a reminder "Life is not a bed of roses." And, in fact, there are those times when life is more like a bed of thorns than roses. Life just simply does not go as it should.

Sometimes, it is much more serious than the humorous illustrations I have given to you. Sometimes, we have to use the sayings more descriptive of the harsh impact such as "The bottom fell out," "The rug was pulled out from under me," or "My world was turned upside down," to help communicate the depth of our confrontation with the painful side of life. At such times, the noise becomes overwhelming—*thump, thump, thump, thump, thump, thump*—and it doesn't seem to ever stop! At such times, the 10 percent of life that is out of round grips our attention and will not let go and we go limping through each day. The questions about survival, or the fairness of life, or about what could have prevented the difficulty come rapid fire into our minds.

Life really, really betrays us and doesn't go as we had planned. I have seen persons who are stunned by death of a loved one, or a relationship that has ended, or news that is too difficult to comprehend, or memories that are coming back that are too intense to handle. I have heard soldiers tell horrific stories of what happened to their buddies or what they did to persons they were fighting. There are things in life that simply should not happen.

Some events should not be a part of humanity, but they are and they always will be, for this world is not as God desires it to be. Now some of us have hope of a new order someday, but as long as we live in this old world, bad events do happen to all persons—and indeed they can. Christians are not excluded as some would falsely have us believe. It has always been so.

There is a determination that promotes our faith and encourages us during such times. Oh, we too may feel that our world is turned upside down. We too have emotions that overwhelm us. We too can be angry at life or God for the hand we have been given. We too can grope around in a stupor and have difficulty finding our way. Now, hear this and hear it clearly: We, as Christians, are not immune from all the tragedies of life; and we are not immune from the emotional and psychological impact as well. Our faith may be shaken, our assumptions shattered, our peace disturbed. Our faith can assist us, but we are human as well.

There are those times in life when all we can do is groan our pain. There are not words. Maybe you have not had such time, and I am happy for you. But you may someday. I have certainly been with persons at such times, and I have had and have some times when words fail me. The pain is too great; the emotions too deep. You hurt and sometimes your heart is breaking, but there is nothing to say. You feel the sensation of your heart breaking, and you cannot find the words to express or there is no one to listen to you struggle for breath and it feels like life will be smothered out. You hear or find certain news, or life surprises you and you are speechless. We attempt to speak, and only the deepest sounds from far within our soul come out in moans and groans of ungodly pain.

Have you ever had experiences such as this? Have you ever been there? I dare say some of you who are reading this are there right now! Always remember that even in any group, large or small, there are some who are in the midst of such hell. That is just another reason we should seek to share love and acceptance. No matter where you are, the person beside you or in front of you or behind you may desperately need your smile or your warm handshake or even your embrace. Never forget that you will truly be a refuge for many a hurting soul.

There are times when our heart aches with the sorrow that can only be released in a groan. Life just doesn't always go as it should. During such times, our deepest longings cannot be put in words.

The good news is what our text for today states for us—that is, during those times when we are speechless because of the tragedies of life, God hears our groans and not only hears them but understands them. Just look at the suffering of Jesus and you will see that God knows about groans and what they mean. God knows the language of groaning.

The passage for today actually states that the spirit uses the language of groans in which the spirit "intercedes for us with groans that words cannot express" (Rom. 8:24). The theologian Paul Tillich wrote, "When we pray we talk to somebody who is not somebody else, but who is nearer to us than we ourselves are."[40] Let that sink in a moment. Tillich also wrote, "It is God Himself who prays through us, when we pray to Him. God Himself in us: that is what Spirit means. Spirit is another word for 'God present.'"[41]

And this is the faith we hold dearly: God hears our groans and is nearer to us than we are to ourselves. God is present. God knows. God cares. God understands. God is there present groaning with us when actual words are not available. The deepest and darkest nights of the soul are understood by our God, and that is the good news. It is good news indeed when there is nothing else to cling to. Hold on to God when there is nothing else—when there are no words to express your pain, when no one else understands. Our God understands and interprets the groans of the soul! This is the God we serve. This is the beauty of our faith!

The Bible says, "We do not know what we ought to pray for but that Spirit himself intercedes with groans or sighs that words cannot express" (Rom. 8:26). Sometimes the feelings are too deep for words. Yes, yes, yes. There is a God in heaven who cares and understands. Cry out to God, even if it is only with great groans and deep moans or even if all you can do is make a whimper! Do so and the spirit will speak for you! This is the God we serve. Amen.

INDEPENDENCE DAY JULY 4TH

As important as the Fourth of July is for those of us in the United States, maybe those of us who claim Christianity need a day to celebrate what seems, to me, to be the essence of our faith: freedom.

Fourth of July

23

Freedom and Independence for the Christian

Preparatory Reading: Galatians 5:1–13

> On July 4 each year, we celebrate our independence in the United States. The freedom in our country is often taken for granted by us, like most things we enjoy on a regular basis. We also have an independence to celebrate in regard to the freedom that we experience as Christians because of the gospel.
>
> Rather than think of the Christian life as a list of dos and don'ts and restrictions as some persons do, the essence, in many ways, of Christianity is freedom. Have you ever considered that? Have you ever had any fireworks go off in your mind or life to celebrate a God who calls you to be spiritually free and enjoy your freedom? Think about it. Welcome to a time of meditation and reflection.

Prayer: Oh, Lord, too often we live in a bondage of our own making yet your desire is that we experience the freedom of the gospel. Free us from ourselves. Amen.

In many areas of the Christian community, Lord knows, there are plenty who will tell you how you should live the Christian life. They will tell you what to do and what not to do. Many flock to such areas of Christianity for they need a structure in their lives and if they can be told what to do and not to do life becomes much simpler. For some, the whole attraction toward Christianity, I am afraid, is this lists of does and don'ts and having someone direct them in what to do.

At the basis of much of this confusion in the Christian community is a view of scripture that is rather different from what existed prior to a few hundred years ago. In some areas, there is an elevation of the scriptures to a place they were never intended to occupy. Now as you know, we take the scriptures seriously and hold them in very high regard. However, for some making the scriptures the literal guidebook for every detail of life is not what they were intended to be. While there are wonderful principles for life in the scriptures, they are not to give us all the answers. The fundamentalists in our land use code words like "Bible-believing Christians" to claim that their way is the only way. Yet, some of us are Bible-believing Christians in a different way.

What this has to do with our topic for today is that a false theology can arise and be promoted by those who use the scriptures in a purely literal way. And good people can fall into the suffocating grip of false beliefs. It camouflages error under the heading of "God's word" or "Bible-believing truth," and many sincere persons walk unknowingly into its quicksand. Most will not drink a bottle labeled Poison, but when it is mixed with food, some will unknowing partake of it.

The apostle Paul states in Galatians 5:1, "It is for freedom that Christ has set us free." What in the world is he talking about? What in the world does he mean?

Well, as always, Paul is writing to a particular group of people who have an issue going on in their church. The agenda in Paul's letters was set by what was going on in that particular situation.

The Christian movement was very young at this time. Most of the Christians were converts from Judaism. In the context of this passage and setting, Paul has heard that there are those who are saying that new converts have to follow all the Jewish law.

The great identifier for Judaism was circumcision. These people had started out well on the Christian walk but were now being influenced by those who are demanding that to be true Christians, the males must be circumcised (v. 7). Now, if I had been a convert at that time and uncircumcised, I am not so sure this demand would have been very influential to me. I think I would have ignored it rather than be circumcised as an adult!

For us today, there is a great principle here. It seems that in all history, there have been those groups who want to add something to the gospel. They want to demand that certain behaviors or certain beliefs be followed or elevated to a status that was never intended.

It usually parades around as something that sounds pretty good on the surface. We are not deceived by counterfeit money if it looks drastically different. If I give you a pink hundred-dollar bill, most of you would notice that there is something not quite right about it. However, if I give you a hundred-dollar bill that is very close in color and everything else to the real thing, you might be deceived by it. Most dangerous theology comes under the disguise of "Bible-believing Christians say this" or "The Bible says" or "It is Biblical" and so on.

But there is an emphasis placed by some theologies that is a wrong, an emphasis placed upon right living according to their code. They do so rather than promoting freedom; we have to become our true selves in the freedom of the gospel. Such theology places the main emphasis upon lifestyle and behavior.

Paul's emphasis here is upon those who require certain behaviors and rituals of Judaism be placed upon the new converts to Christianity. His term for this is "life under the law," and he sees it as subverting Christianity. Applying this to our day, "life under the law" is an emphasis on "measuring up" and determining our status with God by what we do.[42] If we are earnest enough, if we work hard enough, if we are a certain "Bible-believing Christian," if we have enough faith, if we achieve enough, if we view the scriptures in a certain way, then and only then can we really be Christian according to those who place us under the obligation of the law. That is bondage and slavery to what others think and say. It is the gospel of Jesus Christ that is the basis of our standing with God. It is not based on performance but upon the acceptance of God in Christ.

Marcus Borg points out that another scholar calls living under the law living by the "performance principle."[43] The performance principle says that you perform and perform correctly and you can be accepted. You fail to perform and conform to a certain way and you are rejected. That is a life of bondage and never measuring up.

Let me give you a couple of symptoms that this kind of false theology leads to.

(1) Never accepting ourselves. Sometimes this has been called the *real* you versus the *super* you. The super you says, "I have to be someone else in order to be accepted by God and others." So the masks go on. The real you becomes hidden. You cannot be open and honest because you are afraid of rejection. The freedom to be yourself is gone. If we cannot accept ourselves, we cannot feel accepted by God either. But, my friends, the Gospel says, the good news yells to us that God accepts us totally and completely just as we are. In the gospel, there is the good news that we can be honest with our feelings of grief, anger, loneliness, and depression or whatever.

You see, once we come to accept the good news of our acceptance before God, then we begin to receive strength to overcome and we begin to experience the truth of Romans 6:14: "Sin will not have dominion over you for you are not under the law but under grace." In other words, we no longer have to live under the performance principle, wondering if we measure up, but we instead live by the wonderfully freeing news that there is grace enough for all of us.

(2) Legalism. Legalism promotes a rigid emphasis upon external behavior—dos and don'ts and rules and regulations. *Do this and you*

are accepted in this group. Do that and you are rejected. If you do not sign your agreement with our theology, you are rejected or fired or shunned or kept from the inner circle.

Legalism promotes a desperate need for approval. The dos and don'ts start piling up. Our halo has to be adjusted and readjusted according to the persons around us and what they want or desire.

The good news that brings us freedom is not a path of perfect performance. We can never earn God's favor because it is always a gift of love and not based upon what we do. God is pleased with you as you come to him. God loves you regardless of your success or failure in the Christian walk.

(3) *The burden of the "oughts."* The feeling of never doing well enough or being good enough. "I should have, I could have, I would have, if only I could go back and do it over. If only I had not said that." Now all of us realize things we ought to have done, but when we develop a preoccupation with the oughts, this is a problem. We can live in constant turmoil because of what we "should" have done. We can be slaves never accepting our work, our speech, our prayers, our growth as good enough. Only our weaknesses get our attention in such cases. If we always focus on our weaknesses, our strength will deteriorate. Always looking for our oughts will bring despair.

The freedom that comes with the gospel tells us that God accepts us in spite of the things we should have done. Listen to these words by John Wesley:

> Sometimes this excellent quality, tenderness of conscience, is carried to an extreme. We find some who fear where no fear is, who are continually condemning themselves without cause, imagining something to be sinful, where scripture nowhere enjoins it. This is properly termed a scrupulous conscience, and it is a sore evil.[44]

In many ways, we sometimes think that this legalism stuff that Paul writes about is no longer relevant to us. But I believe it will always be relevant, for legalism simply changes its clothing and appears to us in a new form. As I indicated, I believe there is a form of legalism that is growing under the banner of the code words of "Bible believing" and stating "It is Biblical." But elevating the Bible to the status of something to be worshiped instead of a tool to lead us to God is a most subtle and dangerous legalism. For legalism is giving anything—even something good—the place that rightly only belongs to God.

Listen to those words from Paul again: "It is for freedom that Christ has set us free. Stand firm, then and do not let yourselves be burdened again by a yoke of slavery" (Gal. 5:1).

Have you experienced your Christian independence? You are free to be your full potential in Christ. You are free from the uncertainly of trying to live by or measure yourselves by some kind of performance principle. You don't have to measure up—God accepts you in Christ right where you are.

Now, I don't know about you, but that sets off some beautiful and colorful fireworks inside my heart and head. The good news of the gospel is a celebration indeed. Has the celebration begun in your life? Amen.

WORLD COMMUNION SUNDAY

This Holy Day is a reminder of our unity with Christians all over the world and, actually, our unity with all of humanity. Because persons are different, judgment and prejudice should not be in us; and our faith calls us to seek unity, communion, and peace with all.

World Communion Sunday

24

How Wide Is Your Table?
How Big is Your Heart?

Preparatory Reading: Mark 10:2–16

> I don't think we comprehend very well the radical nature of the teachings of Jesus. We have scrubbed his teaching so clean that we have worn off the edges and we have molded them so much into our beliefs that he most likely would not recognize them. But I remain convinced that Jesus was on to something. I remain convinced that Jesus shows us the way of God and the way to God. And I am convinced that Jesus had an extremely radical belief about the importance of relationships and of being gracious and loving to each other.
>
> Do you know this Jesus who challenges you to the depths of your soul? Or do you only know the Jesus that is the watered down, whitewashed, Americanized, and sanitized version that lulls you to sleep and bores you? Think about it. Welcome to a time of reflection and meditation.

Prayer: Oh, God, we so often fail to see the real Jesus. We have made him so much in our image that he has lost his challenge to us. May we somehow, in some way, by the power that comes only by your spirit, see the real Jesus that transforms our lives. We pray that our lives might be touched by the authentic Jesus. Amen.

You may have read or heard this story at some point:

There were two battleships that had been out for training in heavy weather for several days. The visibility was really poor, with patchy fog, so the captain remained at the bridge keeping an eye on all activities.

Shortly after dark, the lookout reported that there was a light straight ahead of their ship. So, the captain asked if it was stationary or moving toward their ship. It was stationary, but they were on a dangerous collision course.

The captain called out for the other ship to be signaled with this message: "I am a captain, we are on a collision course, change course twenty degrees!" Back came the message: "I am a seaman, second class. You had better change your course twenty degrees." For a person of lesser rank than him to respond in this way made the captain furious, so he blurted out as the ships headed toward disaster, "Send this message: 'We are a battleship change your course twenty degrees!'" Back came the message, "I am a lighthouse!" And the captain quickly had his ship change course.[45]

Caleb Rosado, a sociologist, used this illustration to discuss how the captain of the battleship experienced a *paradigm shift*.[46] He had to move away from his initial understanding and from his former way of understanding. For the captain, it had to occur immediately or his ship would have crashed into the rocks and the shore.

When I read this with my bent of thinking, I thought that is what many people experienced when they met Jesus—they had a paradigm shift. The way they had viewed things in the past had to change. The old way would no longer do. And I think we too often fail to appreciate how dramatic a change Jesus called for people to make.

That is why Nicodemus came to Jesus, struggling with what to do, and having difficulty understanding the transformation Jesus called for. That is why the Pharisees, who were so loyal to the status quo, hated Jesus and could not make the shift with him. That is why even the disciples of Jesus took so long to comprehend that he was calling them to a new way of living. That is why the Pharisees came to Jesus and asked him about divorce and then when they were in the house again, it says that the disciples of Jesus asked him about the question of divorce again. And by the way, Jesus allowed an exception to the command not to divorce. He upheld the permanence of marriage; however, he recognized there are exceptions and here he goes against the then current ability of men to find all kinds of silly exceptions to divorce and leave a woman destitute in that culture.

Jesus protected the vulnerable. This is why they tried to keep the little children from coming to Jesus and rebuked them, which made Jesus indignant. He got mad, and said to let the little children come to him and then he took the children in his arms.

You see, don't you? Jesus called for a new way of relating, and it was not just a twenty-degree change of course; it was a radical turnaround and a complete change of direction. Jesus called and continues to call for paradigm shifts in our thinking, in our beliefs, and in our lives.

Now, let me write very plainly for a moment. I worked as a minister for twenty years and repeated over and over again the importance of relationship as followers of Jesus, but some never heard and just wrote it off as a naïve understanding. However, I believe one cannot get around the fact that Jesus called us to relate in a new way, a better way; and if we do not get that right, nothing else matters very much. I dare say, some who thought I was so repetitive were the very ones who had never really heard this message of Jesus about transforming relationships. It is difficult to penetrate certain established ways of thinking.

Jesus called for us to have a relationship with God. And that can only happen if we come to really believe in a God of love and grace. Oh, you can maybe outwardly change your behavior at least for a while, if you have a concept of an angry and vengeful God. But that has nothing to do with what Jesus called us to do.

On World Communion Sunday, we must consider the table of our Lord and what we as disciples of Jesus believe about the table. I believe in the open table. In my ministry, I emphasized many times this truth: You do not have to have any degree to come to the table. You can be smart or not so smart. You can be short or tall. You can be skinny or not so skinny. You can be rich or poor, and yet there is room at the table for you. You can do things rather well or you can be a person who blows it often and you are still invited.

Jesus taught us that God does not set up barriers and that God welcomes all. And let me even push it more and ask you, Who do we not want at the table? Whom do you want to exclude? These are serious questions with which to struggle.

Now, of course, we have those whom we have some boundaries with such as those who are dangerous or those who are destructive. And sometimes, we have to set limits with negative persons in our lives that is proper and healthy.

However, that is not what I am talking about. I am talking about people that we choose to look down upon, persons we want to exclude. Many times, we want to be around people only like us, but we are all different and no two are exactly alike so that can be a very lonely tactic. I think it is pretty clear that God loves variety and so should we.

The religious leaders of Jesus's day excluded many, and they were upset that Jesus included sinners and prostitutes and tax collectors. Can you imagine the uproar he caused? What if we took the position that we were going to truly welcome all who come seeking God? Would we be ready? Would we be able to do it?

You know what? I can answer that. I am sure we are not ready. We are not ready for the dramatic paradigm shift or the movement to be as inclusive as Jesus.

Now think about it. Here is my question for us: Are we ready to be as inclusive as Jesus? Let me suggest to you that I believe there are plenty of people who are looking for people to love them just as they are and to care for them and to include them. Oh, they may be considered misfits by some but not by God.

Now hear this: I once pastored a church that was built over a hundred years ago. It was built out of the marble that was actually, to put it in biblical terms, stones that the builders rejected! They could not be used in the normal construction projects. In other words, the stones were misfits and leftovers and rejects! And they said of Jesus that he was the stone the builders rejected.

Another part of my history is that the first church I pastored was in Chicago and we had all sorts of persons who found God at our church. We had a guy who had run a chop shop for stolen cars, we had an ex-con, we had many different ethnic groups and races and we grew, and some of the Christians in the area were jealous or threatened or something.

Later, word got to me that someone said that our church was where the misfits went. Well, my response was, "Amen! Misfits need a church too, and if they want to call us that, so be it. I wouldn't even mind putting out a sign that reads 'The Church for Misfits' or 'The Church for Rejects' for we have all been rejected at some time or another."

What if all churches were truly places where all could find acceptance and a place to grow with God? What if we were open to those who are rejected by others and who are ostracized by others? You know what we would be doing? We would be following the way of Jesus. We really would be. But are we courageous enough? Are we brave enough? Are we strong enough? Can we take the risk to go the Jesus way, or will we play it safe and crash into the status quo rocks and the sticky mud of doing church the same old way?

What is your desire? Do you want to step out in faith or do you want to hold on what most everyone else is doing? Churches often struggle to truly be the church of Jesus and be truly accepting.

Well, I went in a different direction that I had assumed when I started this chapter. (Ha!) However, it comes from my heart, and I hope the spirit of God had some direction in it. This is what God has put in my heart for us.

And I think the last part of our scripture reading about children is applicable here. Just as Jesus broke down the barriers for the children and open his arms to them, I think he does for all persons, for each and every person is a child of God.

On World Communion Sunday, I challenge us all to think and to question if our table is wide enough to include all and if our heart is big enough to love everyone.

I am suggesting that we be willing to change course before it is too late. I am suggesting that we be willing to change course to have a greater ministry. I suggesting that we invite all to come to our table and that we do not hinder any of them, for the kingdom of God belongs and is open to all.

My prior church that I mentioned became a beautiful building by receiving and incorporating all the misfit marble blocks just as churches will become beautiful congregations if we will but accept all the so-called misfits around us. Are you ready? Are you willing to take the risk? Is your heart large enough? Is my heart large enough? Can we make room at our table or does Jesus have to sit with the excluded and rejected persons all by himself? Amen.

ALL SAINTS DAY

We are not alone. There are those who have gone before us and who will come after us. We remember those who have contributed to our lives on this day and the connections we still maintain with them, and we consider that we are passing the baton to those who come after us.

All Saints' Day

25

When Is the Last Time You Saw a Saint?

Preparatory Reading: Hebrews 12:1–3

All Saints' Day is a day we remember the saints who have walked before us. What is a saint anyway? Can you be alive and on this earth and be a saint? Or do you have to somehow sprout wings before you are a saint?

Do saints laugh? Do they ever cry? Do we have to go to museums or dusty old books with faded pictures to see the saints? Where would you go to find a saint? Think about it. Welcome to a time of reflection and meditation.

Prayer: Oh, God, this thing called the Christian life sometimes confuses us. For we look at ourselves and our faults and failures and wonder what it is all about. But help us to turn our eyes to Jesus and realize that when we march with him, we are and will be marching into your kingdom. In his name, we pray. Amen.

Some time ago now, I was going through the checkout line at the grocery store and noticed the picture and headline on one of the magazines they put out that has sensational, attention-grabbing material. There he was in a wheelchair, Elvis, appropriately aged, but there was Elvis! I cannot remember the headline, but I am sure it was something like "Elvis Found Alive!" Or "Elvis Hidden All These Years" or something like that. Some of us can still recall when Elvis Presley died and later when there were "sightings" of him, some down at the local Kmarts. Well, I suppose such are just symptoms of our society longing not to lose some of the people who have become important to us. By the way, it is true that Elvis is still making a pretty hefty income each year, so in some ways he does live on and on.

However, what I want to get to is what about any "sighting" you have had not of Elvis but of God's saints down at Kmart or maybe at Wal-Mart. Have you ever sighted any saints around town?

Have you ever seen a saint? Do they somehow appear different? Do they have a halo or some kind of aura around them? Do they walk with a Bible in hand? Are they religious all the time? How about this: Can you picture a saint laughing or going to a party or having a fun time?

After all, saints are saints, and that is all there is too it. They have almost sprouted wings of angels to some. Ever see any saints down at Kmart? Would a saint ever get excited about a Blue Light Special? What do saints eat anyway? Do they even need to eat? Do they sleep, or are they too busy doing the work of God twenty-four seven?

What is a saint? How would you define or describe a saint? Any saints at Kmart, Wal-Mart, or what about the church? Any saints in the church? Now, if I ask the opposite, it might be easier. Any devils in the church?

We could point out some devils, I'm sure! But today, I am asking, Are there any saints in the church, today, right now, even here among us? If I asked all the saints to stand up, how many would there be? Any, none, one, two, fifteen?

Well, when Paul wrote his letters to the churches, he addressed them to the saints of a particular place—"To the saints at Ephesus," "To the saints at Corinth," "To the saints at Philippi," "To the saints at Colossae." Was Paul writing to one or two persons at each place? No, he was writing to the whole church. Do you get it? The church is full of saints!

You are a saint! Wow? Would that change your definition of what a saint is? You may have to adjust the halo a bit or maybe remove it from your definition. We know that the churches to whom Paul was writing were not filled with members who were perfect. There was bickering among them, there were many problems in them, and their humanity was often showing—yet they are called saints.

Well, what do you make of that? Saints are not just those who make a big splash for God or are well known. The great preacher Peter Marshall once did a sermon on Andrew and called him the "Saint of the Rank and File."[47] In other words, Andrew was a saint among the ordinary. He was an ordinary person. There are those who are identified in particular ways as saints, but this is not the only way to identify saints.

Can you identify yourself as a saint? A saint is simply one who had expressed faith in Jesus Christ. It has nothing to do with perfection. Saints have flesh and blood and are filled with the contradictions and conflicts that are the lot of humanity. Do you get it? You are a saint!

You see, I believe that if you recognize who you are as a child of God and are affirmed in that identity, you will be more likely to live that identity than if you have some impossible standard put before you that is based on fantasy or unreality or mythology. If you put the model so far out that no one thinks they can obtain it, it is useless in some ways. But if you begin by giving people the identity, then they have a calling to live in that identity. Like the toy store that says Toys "R" Us—Saints "R" Us! Can you believe it? We are saints set aside by God to live for him in spite of all our failings and faults. We are saints!

A bishop of Sweden once said, "Saints are those who make it easier for us to believe in God."[48] Well, maybe so. Because many persons make it easier for me to believe in God as they hang with God through all the trials and tribulations of everyday life. Robert Louis Stevenson said, "Saints are sinners who keep on going."[49] That is us, and that is the greatest witness of the work of God in our lives: we keep on going, and we keep on looking unto Jesus as our text said.

On All Saints' Day, let's remember those who have walked before us, especially those who have walked right in front of us, who have been in our churches or in our families. There are saints we have and do rub shoulders with. They are among us and have lived among us. What are they saying to us? What have some who have gone before you said to you with their words or their lives?

How have they contributed to your faith? I think of one saint who was ninety-two years old at the time of her death and still following God with such inspiration. I ran into a saint down at Home Depot—and there are saints even at Home Depot—who had a hope for great things and great possibilities. He saw people and life by faith, and his faith energizes my faith even now. I think of all the "rank and file"—to use Peter Marshall's words as mentioned above—who kept on keeping on through all kinds of difficulties. I think of minister mentors who were saints and who encouraged me along the path and spoke words of comfort and encouragement. Who are the saints who influenced you? Think of saints who have been in your life, remember them.

We have saints remembered, those who have gone before us and call us to hold on to the faith, that great cloud of witnesses that calls us to live the Christian life. They were not perfect, but they loved God and made a difference.

Don't you realize that the saints who have gone before us are holding out the baton? They are telling us that we are to throw off everything that hinders and the sin that so easily entangles us and let us run with perseverance the race marked out for us! Will you grab hold of the baton? Don't let it drop. Hold on to the baton and run! Run the race! Stay on course with Jesus. Run the race! Take the baton!

What do you want to have remembered about your sainthood? When you pass off the baton to the next generation of saints, what

do you want to leave with them? What kind of faith are we presenting for them? On this note, Mary Anderson wrote this:

> Will we leave a legacy of justice or will we leave a
> bequest of selfishness? ... Those we admire as witnesses
> to Christ [*saints of Christ*] are our best examples of liv-
> ing the simple commands of Jesus to love God with our
> whole selves and our neighbor as ourselves...It means
> forgiving, not judging, loving, not despising; lifting up,
> not tearing down.[50]

We are called to be saints. Will we not grab hold of the baton
from those who have gone before us and continue on in the way they
have modeled for us?

Yes, there are saints at Kmart, Wal-Mart, and even—yes, even—
in the church! Amen.

THANKSGIVING

When we fail to incorporate thankfulness into our lives, we are missing a component of joy. As we appreciate what we have, our focus can shift, and we see all that we have anew and our lives become more positive. This is good medicine for the soul.

Thanksgiving

26

Are You Taking the Proper Dosage of Thankfulness for the Journey?

Preparatory Reading: 1 Thessalonians 5:16–18

Charles Spurgeon wrote back in the 1800s, "The best music of a Christian consists in thankfulness to God."[51]

Are you making any of this kind of music for God. I hope that we can become a more thankful people this Thanksgiving. Think about it. Welcome to a time of meditation and reflection.

Prayer: Oh, God, we seemed to operate out of a mentality of scarcity, and so we focus on what we need and what we don't have instead of the abundance we have. May we pause long enough during this season to be thankful for the blessings we enjoy. Move us to be a more thankful people. For we pray in the spirit of Christ. Amen.

I once wrote in a church newsletter, when our children were small, that one of the greatest fears about my children was that they would grow up and not be thankful. Children reveal to us the difficulties of humanity so well. It is like the woman who was attempting to instill in her son politeness and thankfulness and it didn't work out

183

as she planned. Her son was given an orange by a man, so the mom asked of her son, "What do you say to this nice man?" The little fellow thought a moment and then handed the orange back to the man and said, "Peel it!"

Somehow, the concept of being thankful can elude us as children. However, it also happens to adults. Thanksgiving is a nice reminder for us each year, if we allow it to be. And I want to suggest today that thankfulness is one of those positive psychological principles that the Bible supports and encourages.

I love this story: The day before Thanksgiving, an elderly man in Phoenix called his son in New York and said to him, "I hate to ruin your day, but I have to tell you that your mother and I are divorcing. Forty-five years of misery is enough. We're sick of each other, and so you call your sister in Chicago and tell her."

Frantic, the son called his sister, who exploded on the phone. "Like heck they're getting divorced," she shouted, "I'll take care of this."

She called Phoenix immediately and said to her father, "You are *not* getting divorced. Don't do a single thing until I get there. I'm calling my brother back, and we'll both be there tomorrow. Until then, don't do a thing. *Do you hear me?*"

The man hung up his phone and turned to his wife. "Okay, honey. The kids are coming for Thanksgiving and paying for their flights!"

Thanksgiving is a time for getting together, and this couple had the importance of togetherness in mind, even if they were a bit manipulative with their children. It may be that we can do better with Thanksgiving when we are thankful with others. But too often we operate out of a mentality of scarcity and so we eat like that also. We are starving and we stuff ourselves like there will be no food tomorrow, and we somehow forget the abundance and excessiveness of our lives. Shall we not take time to be thankful? Shall we not pause in our hectic and frantic pace and count our blessings? It would be good for our mental, spiritual, and physical health to do so.

Someone compiled this list of questions you can ask to test whether you are a grateful person or not:

1. Which do you tend to talk about more, your blessings, or your disappointments?
2. Are you a complainer, always grumbling, always finding fault with your circumstances?
3. Are you content with what you have or always dissatisfied and wanting more?
4. Do you find it easier to count your blessings, or is it easier to count your afflictions?
5. Do you express thanks to others when they help you, or do you just take it as your due?
6. Would others say that you are a thankful person?

Such questions challenge most of us, do they not? Our focus slips to the negative side of life all too often.

Dr. Dale Robbins writes,

> I used to think people complained because they had a lot of problems. But I have come to realize that they have problems because they complain. Complaining doesn't change anything or make situations better. It amplifies frustration, spreads discontent and discord, and can invoke an invitation for the devil to cause havoc with our lives.[52]

And when we are not thankful, we often become complainers and whiners.

Two schoolteachers who hadn't seen each other in several years met at a convention. They began filling each other in on what had happened in their lives since the last time they had visited together. One teacher said, "I got married two years ago."

"Oh, that's good," her friend replied.

"Well, no, not really," the first one said. "My husband is twice as old as I am."

"Oh, that's bad," her friend replied.

"Well, no, not really," she said, "because he is a millionaire several times over."

"Oh, that's good," her friend replied.

"Well, no, not really," she said, "because he turned out to be mean, and he won't give me any money at all."

"Oh, that's bad," her friend replied.

"Well, no, not really," she said. "He did build us a three-hundred-thousand-dollar house."

"Oh, that's good," her friend replied.

"Well, no, not really," she said. "It burned down last month."

"Oh, that's bad," her friend replied.

"Well, no, not really," she said. "He was in it when it burned down!"

Much of how we see life is based on perspective, isn't it? Now, I am not saying the lady in this story had the best perspective, but it is a humorous way to make us think about how we think and how that colors our view of circumstances.

Listen to how one person turned their thinking upside down:

I am thankful for:
- the taxes I pay because it means I'm employed;
- the clothes that fit a little too snug because it means I have enough to eat;
- all the complaining I hear about our government because it means we have freedom of speech;
- the lady behind me in church who sings off key because it means that I can hear;
- the piles of laundry and ironing because it means my loved ones are nearby; and
- the alarm that goes off in the early morning hours because it means that I'm alive.[53]

These push a bit far; however, you get the concept! Indeed, 1 Thessalonians 5:16–18 is a fantastic passage for Thanksgiving. Listen to what it says: "Be joyful always. Pray continually. Give thanks in all circumstances for this is God's will for you in Christ Jesus."

Now, you need to realize that it doesn't say "Give thanks *for* all circumstances" but, rather, "*In* all circumstances."

That is positive psychology. There is a term in psychology called *capitalization* that means that one tells others about positive events in his or her life. It is like the word says—*capitalization* is putting your blessings in capital letters and sharing or telling them to others. And you know what has been found when you use capitalization of the good events in your life? The research article I read put it this way: "Telling others about positive events in one's life—is likely to generate additional positive affect over and above positive affect associate with the event itself."[54]

So when you count your blessing that is good and if you share the news of good events with others, it even enhances the good feelings you get from what has happened. We need to share the good things that happen to us and not focus on all the bad and frustrating events of our lives.

What did the apostle Paul write? He reveals to us that when we are thankful, we will find a special kind of peace. He encourages us to think on positive things (to capitalized on them, if you please), and he reveals to us that when we do this, we can be like him and be content even in difficult circumstances. Look again to his words in Philippians 4:6–12 and note these concepts.

I challenge each of us to pause a moment during this season and be thankful for all that we have and be thankful for what matters to us most in life. Pause and be thankful and share that thankfulness with your God and with others. Capitalize your blessings in big, bold letters and keep them before you and share them with those around you and you will find yourselves to be even more blessed.

May we truly be a thankful people this Thanksgiving! Amen.

27

Gratitude Can Change an Attitude!

Preparatory Reading: Philippians 4:4–13

> Are we a thankful people? What would happen if we truly incorporated thanksgiving into the depths of our being? What does thanksgiving promote in our lives? What does an attitude of gratitude promote in our lives? Think about it. Welcome to a time of reflection and meditation.

Prayer: Oh, God, in this land of plenty, we too often become smug in our comfort zones for we have so much and we have very anorexic words of thanksgiving. We pray that our words of thanksgiving have some meat on them, that we might have an attitude of gratitude and appreciation for the great blessings we enjoy. May we learn how to rejoice and be thankful, in the name of Jesus, we pray. Amen.

How often do we say "He has an attitude" or "She has an attitude"? It has gotten to where we do not even have to add an adjective in order to know what we mean. When we say "He has an attitude," we automatically know it is a bad attitude and we had better stand clear. A person gets up in the morning with an attitude, and we know they got up on the wrong side of the bed. A person has an attitude at work, and everyone attempts to stay clear of them. A person has an attitude at church, and we all reach out to them to see what's going on—well, maybe not.

Let me make a suggestion to you, something I have observed, and it is this: It is difficult to have an attitude, a bad attitude, if we are thankful. A grateful heart produces a good attitude. Gratitude can change "an attitude." Gratitude can give you a positive attitude. If you are thankful for a new day when you wake up, that equals to a better attitude. If you find something to be thankful for in most every part of life, it adds up to a better attitude.

Even if you burn the turkey this on Thanksgiving, you can have a good attitude, as someone said, by thinking of something positive like, "Hey, I won't have to eat turkey sandwiches for three weeks." Can you pull that off?

Remember Viktor Frankl? He was the concentration camp survivor who wrote, "Everything can be taken from a man [*or woman*] but one thing: the last of human freedoms—to choose one's attitude in any given set of circumstances, to choose one's way."[55]

As we come to our scripture for today, it is a passage pregnant with many positive thoughts. As I was studying it, something new came to me. Remember Paul has written earlier in this letter (Phil. 2:5) that our attitude should be the same as that of Christ Jesus. And what hit me this week is that our passage is another way Paul is giving to us to have the attitude of Christ. Therefore, I would like to pull a few points from our passage that show how an attitude of gratitude can promote this Christlikeness in our lives.

First of all, an attitude of gratitude promotes joy. Note Philippians 4:4 and that Paul is speaking from prison, and he says in Philippians 4:10 that he rejoices so he is also setting an example of this kind of joy. This is not just some fleeting feeling but a consistent, abiding joy that comes from our relationship with Christ—"Rejoice in the Lord," it is said in Philippians 4:4. It is a joy that can take the edge off for it produces a forbearance and gentleness, which says, "Let your gentleness be evident to all" (Phil. 4:4b).

Paul states a truth here that helps us maintain the joy: "the Lord is at hand. The early Christians lived with a sense that Christ was still present with them. Do you want to maintain joy in your life? Live with the reality that God is near to you. Are you anxious about life and living? Live with the reality that God walks with you through all of life. So, first of all, an attitude of gratitude promotes joy.

Second, an attitude of gratitude promotes thankfulness. He ties these together in Philippians 4:5. Gratitude promotes thankfulness in our talks with God. With an attitude of gratitude, we do not just pray to God and plead with God with our petitions; we also talk to God with thankfulness. Now that can change an attitude. How often do we really thank our God, or are we more expert at simply asking for things all the time? What percentage of our talks with God are thanksgiving and what percentage are "God, 'I want'" or "God, 'I need'"?

I once heard a good illustration from John Ortberg. I believe he is a minister in Chicago. He told of a *Peanuts* comic by Charles Schulz where Snoopy was musing as he lay on his doghouse on Thanksgiving Day. Snoopy is angry and has a bad attitude because Charlie Brown and his family are having a turkey and dressing and all the thanksgiving feast inside, and Snoopy only has dog food to eat. Snoopy is very upset until he changes his attitude and thinks, *It could be worse. I could have been born a turkey!*

John emphasizes those words, "It could be worse." Then he says, "When you get into your car and you are tempted to feel 'I could be happy if I had a new car,' say 'It could be worse.'" When you get home and you walk into your house and you will be tempted to think, *I could be happier if I had a bigger and more expensive home*, say, "It could be worse." What will you say?

Then he said, "When you wake up in the morning and you roll over and you see your spouse I want you to say, 'No, no don't do that one!'" That is a great story he tells. So always remember "it could be worse" and be thankful for what you have. An attitude of gratitude promotes thankfulness.

Third, an attitude of gratitude promotes the contemplation of the good and positive. Philippians 4:8 encourages us to focus on the good and beautiful. An attitude of gratitude promotes "beautifulizing," to coin a term. In the therapy field, we talk of some who are good at "awfulizing."

Some time ago, *Readers Digest* had a good illustration of this:

> Both the hummingbird and the vulture fly over our nation's deserts. All vultures see is rotting meat, because that is what they look for. They thrive on that diet. But hummingbirds ignore the smelly flesh of dead animals. Instead, they look for the colorful blossoms of desert plants. The vultures live on what was. They live on the past. They fill themselves with what is dead and gone. But hummingbirds live on what is. They seek new life. They fill themselves with freshness and life. Each bird finds what it is looking for. We all do.[56]

And the question for us today is, Are we a vulture in life always looking for the dead, the putrefying, the ugly, the nasty, the destructive in life, or are we seeking the things Paul says in Philippians 4:8? It makes a difference what we focus upon!

Do you think in a positive way or a negative way? Remember the negative thinking of the Hebrews when they saw Goliath, "Why, he's too big for us to fight"? David looked at Goliath and focused on the positive and said, "He's too big to miss." An attitude of gratitude promotes the contemplation of good and positive. Try it and see what happens in your life!

Our fourth point is that an attitude of gratitude promotes positive modeling. In Philippians 4:9, Paul says, "Whatever you have learned or received or heard or seen in me—put into practice." How many of us can say "Whatever you have heard from me, imitate"?

When he was eight years old, I was helping our son Ben build a rabbit "gum"—or, at least, that is what we called them when I was a boy. It is a trap to catch a rabbit that does not hurt the rabbit. It is a box that has wire screen on one end and a trap door on the other. When the rabbit enters, it goes back in the box toward some food and as it does so, it hits a stick that makes the door close.

Anyway, as we are building the rabbit gum, I was talking to Ben about getting the boards flush, or lining them up smoothly. I said, "Ben, this is called getting the board flush." Then I continued, "It is not so important on a rabbit gum, but if you were building a house, you would want them to be flush." I showed him how to do it as I talked.

Later that same day, my wife told me the following, and it brought tears to my eyes. Ben was piddling in the barn, building something, and he called for Debbie to assist him. Then he said, "Now try to get the board flush. It doesn't matter so much when you are building something like this, but if you were building a house, it would be important." Wow! People do learn from our example, especially our children. I fail and falter so often as a parent, but on that day, I felt proud of being an example.

We are much more comfortable with "do as I say," not "as I do." But we need to fill our lives with positive persons—those who have the proper attitude, those we can imitate. Most of all, of course, this is to see Jesus as an example for us. Again, remember Paul said, "Your attitude should be the same as that of Christ Jesus" (Phil. 2:5). Not in the sense that we see Jesus and feel the model is beyond reach or some perfectionistic way but that the model calls forth from us the qualities the model exhibits.

Last, an attitude of gratitude promotes contentment and peace (Phil. 4:7, 11–13). Now this is fantastic, don't miss it. This is why we are all seeking peace and contentment. Note that Paul says that he has "learned to be content whatever the circumstances" (v. 11). Does this mean that on the Damascus Road, when he met Christ he had peace and contentment at that instant? Well, maybe in some sense.

But he is saying that he has had to learn contentment. Therefore, our attitude can be learned. Some of us have to unlearn a negative attitude and have to continually grow in the attitude of gratitude.

But there is hope here. Erma Bombeck gave an illustration back in the early 1990s:

> An estimated 1.5 million people are living today after bouts with breast cancer. Every time I forget to feel grateful to be among them, I hear the voice of an eight-year-old named Christina, who had cancer of the nervous system. When asked what she wanted for her birthday, she thought long and hard and finally said, "I don't know. I have two sticker books and a Cabbage Patch doll. I have everything!" The kid is right.[57]

And Paul says in verse 12 that this comes with learning to have the mind of Christ. This comes with learning to walk with Christ. This comes from keeping everything in proper perspective. This comes with having an attitude like Christ. Listen to these words by an unknown author:

Be thankful that you don't already have everything you desire.
If you did, what would there be to look forward to?
Be thankful when you don't know something,
for it gives you the opportunity to learn.
Be thankful for the difficult times. During those times you grow.
Be thankful for your limitations,
because they give you opportunities for improvement.
Be thankful for each new challenge,
because it will build your strength and character.
Be thankful for your mistakes. They will teach you valuable lessons.
Be thankful when you're tired and weary,
because it means you've made a difference.
It's easy to be thankful for the good things.

A life of rich fulfillment comes to those who
are also thankful for the setbacks.
Gratitude can turn a negative into a positive.
Find a way to be thankful for your troubles,
and they can become your blessings.

An attitude of gratitude really can promote contentment and peace in our lives. It can give us quiet restfulness in our souls.

Yes, gratitude can change an attitude. And an attitude of gratitude can promote great and positive things in our lives and bring us closer to having the attitude of Christ. Thanks be to God for Christ Jesus and his continued work in our lives. May God help us have an attitude of gratitude this Thanksgiving season and all the year through. Amen.

THE SEASON OF ADVENT

During this season, we celebrate the birth of Jesus and we recall the virtues Jesus gave to us. What a gift came to us wrapped up in swaddling clothes! He gifted us with a way to live in relation to God and a call to love in deeper and fuller manner. We have included the following for this season:

- First Sunday of Advent—Hope
- Second Sunday of Advent—Peace
- Third Sunday of Advent—Joy
- Fourth Sunday of Advent—Love
- The Longest Night (The Winter Solstice)
- Christmas Eve
- Christmas

The Season of Advent

28

First Sunday of Advent Prepare for the Journey toward Hope!

Preparatory Reading: Mark 1:1–9

> Well, this is the first Sunday of Advent. What does Advent mean to you? Does it have anything special about it? Or does this time of year come with such regularity and monotony and we have gone through it so many times that is just so ordinary for us? What do you expect, if anything, from this season? Think about it. Welcome to a time of meditation and reflection.

Prayer: Oh God the danger is that you will come and we will miss your coming or that you will come and our lives will continue on untouched. Oh Lord, may your voice get our attention and call us to you this day is our prayer, in the name of the Christ Child, Amen

We have now been plopped down into the Advent season. Many of us have a love/hate or at least have a love/dislike with this time of year. I have already heard some say some emphatic words like "I hate the Christmas season!" and "I will be glad when it is all over." It is sad but true. We struggle with this season because somehow, we have allowed ourselves to get into a hyperactive, senseless hurrying from one activity to another, all the while nibbling at high-calorie and high fat "munchables and crunchables." And pretty soon, we feel like overstuffed Santas and with our bellies about to explode and we have overstuffed schedules as well.

By the way, do you know how someone has described the history of a man's life? He begins by believing in Santa Claus, and then he evolves to disbelieving in Santa Claus. Finally, lo and behold, he *becomes* Santa Claus. And we wonder why men have middle age crises! I believe it is all because of the phenomena of Santa Claus. It is all very confusing. It is confusing to all of us for, at times, the very season of giving and receiving has so distorted and perverted the key concepts and behaviors of the Christian life.

Therefore, we do struggle in some ways with this season, and it is not all bad that we struggle, for nothing in life is really that simple. We only have to sort it all out. There is something about life that offers us the opportunity to choose at least some of our path. We can choose all this craziness or we can set limits so that we keep some measure of sanity. The difficult struggle for me is that I have to be honest and tell you that I already had a couple of the negative thoughts about the season myself before I even got to this first Sunday of Advent. However, we pause and consider that the Advent Season is to help us focus upon some virtues Jesus brought to us.

It is vital that we all come to our scripture today and come to our God today with an openness to what God wants to say to us during the Advent Season this year. Otherwise, we will not hear God's voice above the chatter and clamor of the secularization of the Advent season. It is then important for us to hear the call of John the Baptist, the nonconformist, calling out to us. Mark applies the words from Isaiah to John the Baptist: "A voice of one calling in the desert [*or wilderness*]" (Mark 1:3). One understanding of the wilderness, or desert, is as a place of danger and of separation from God as, we at times, discuss during the Lenten Season.

When John the Baptist comes as a "a voice of one calling in the desert," maybe is it not too far a stretch to imagine how much we need a voice calling to us in the wilderness of our own confused, mindless, and godless modern world. For our modern world is indeed a wilderness of sorts. Maybe his cry should be seen as a microcosm of what our own society needs.

We need a "a voice of one calling in the desert [or *wilderness*]" (Mark 1:3) to give us guidance and to direct our pathways during the complex and competing and chaotic days of the Christmas wilderness. I don't mean to be negative about how we observe Christmas; however, I am attempting to be a small voice of challenge to us this morning. Otherwise, we may not hear what we need to hear this season.

Ponder on these thoughts:

- I need a voice calling or shouting to me in the wilderness at Advent to give me guidance, don't I?
- I need a voice calling or shouting to me in the wilderness at Advent, a voice that will give me some direction through the maze so that I will end up at the right place, don't I?
- I need a voice calling or shouting to me in the wilderness at Advent to bring my focus to what really matters rather than the voices of the many fighting for my attention at this time of year, don't I?

We need a voice to lead us to Christ's voice. We need a voice to lead us to the Messiah—the voice of a better way.

Therefore, let us very briefly note some ways that John the Baptist spoke to the people of his day who were in a very different culture from us, but perhaps the human condition today is not so different in some ways. Let's notice how John the Baptist helps us with preparation. He calls us to

- prepare the way or a way for the Lord,

- prepare for repentance, and
- prepare for the coming of hope.

First of all, prepare the way or a way for the Lord. The historical setting of words like these was when the people literally had to prepare for the visit of a king. They had to literally make straight paths for him. The messenger announced the news of the kings coming and told the people to literally clear a path for him. The road might be blocked by various things. Boulders might be in the way and fallen trees might obstruct the pathway. Potholes might make the way too difficult. My friends, if we are to make way for the Christ to come into our lives, I wonder what needs to be cleared out of the way to prepare for his coming. I wonder if there are any obstacles in our hearts that are in the way?

John the Baptist comes in the tradition of the prophet Elijah to announce the good news. He comes as "a voice crying aloud in the wilderness" to "prepare the way for the Lord." Can you hear him speaking to you this morning? What is blocking the reception of the Christ child into your life? What do you need to clear out of the way in order to be able to receive the salvation offered there in the lowly manger? I challenge each of us to prepare the way for him to come to us.

Second, John the Baptist comes as "a voice crying aloud in the wilderness," crying above all the background noise of our lives, calling us to prepare for repentance. Notice in Luke 21:34 what Jesus says about being prepared: "Be careful, or your hearts will be weighed down with dissipation, drunkenness, and the anxieties of life."

It is so easy for us to be unprepared and especially today in this area. Repentance—who, me? Why should I need repentance? That is an outdated concept, isn't it? Well, no it isn't. It is as relevant as when John preached it and maybe even more so for today we do not even recognize our need. In verse 4, John came preaching a baptism of repentance.

There are various words in the scriptures that have to do with the old concept called sin, and these words have to do with our life experience such as with such as "missing the mark," "to act wrongly," and "to rebel." The major concept appears to be that of going against God's will.[58] Do you know anyone with known experience of going against God's will? Do you know of anyone in need of repentance in order to be able to truly receive the Christ this advent season?

Keep in mind these words by Barbara Brown Taylor:

...the choice to remain in wrecked relationship with God and other human beings is called sin. The choice to enter into the process of repair is called repentance, an often-bitter medicine with the undisputed power to save lives.[59]

She goes on to say that "sin is not simply a set of behaviors to be avoided...not the violation of laws but the violation of relationships." Therefore, she states the restoration of relationship is the key emphasis.

Repentance is that restoration. Don't you like the words she uses, "The process of repair is called repentance"? The process of repair of a wrecked relationship is called repentance. Anybody reading these words today need repair of a wrecked relationship? With God? With someone else? Repentance is that reparation process. Don't put it off. John the Baptist would say "Do it today," I believe. Prepare for repentance and thereby allow Jesus to be born anew in your life!

Once at night, I heard a noise in front of the parsonage in Florida and went out front to check out what was happening. I could barely see a light just down in the ravine in front of the house. I ran over and a pickup truck was almost straight down in the ravine, with the motor still running. After calling 911, I tried to reach the driver. I had difficulty getting to the truck because of the steepness and the brushes and briers all around it.

I was finally able to get to the bed of the pickup and slid down it to the cab. Inside was a semiconscious man, and as I reached in over him to cut off the engine, I noticed that he was clutching a wad of money. Even during his accident, he continued to clutch on to his money.

Some of us have gotten into a semiconscious state where we are not in touch with real life and we clutch on to money and other items instead of the important things of life. It is time to get on track with what matters. It is not that money or many other things are bad, but if we are clutching on to them so tightly that our relationships, our health, and our spiritual lives are ignored, it is time to make a change, to repent.

Last, John is a voice calling loudly in the wilderness for us to prepare for hope. What a wonderful word *hope* is. It is a burst of energy into a dead life. It is a ray of sunlight in a storm. A little bit of this medicine will cure a hospital full of ills.

Anyone need a dose of hope? Maybe you even need some hope that you can make it through this season alive. Maybe the sadness of the season has covered hope with a black cloud. Maybe you need some hope that God really does love you. Maybe you need some hope that life really can be different. This was the message of John the Baptist. He is announcing the coming of Christ.

Christ was a long-awaited hope. For centuries, the Hebrews had looked forward to a messiah, a savior, and a hope for the present and the future. Christ was that hope for many, and he can be that hope for us. He revealed that we can have an experience of God that is a relationship. We can know him and have the spirit move in our lives to give us meaning and purpose and guidance. We can have hope of companionship with God now and forever. What a hope and a reality that can be!

The message of Christianity is that we are to have hope. Let us enter the advent season with the expectancy of finding hope for today and tomorrow. In the midst of the wilderness of our age, there is still the beacon star of Christ to point us to hope! There is still "a voice crying aloud in the wilderness," the wilderness of our own perverse generation. The voice is calling in the tradition of John the Baptist to prepare us to receive the Christ Child this Advent Season.

What is that voice saying to you? What does that voice need to say to you? What do you need to hear from that voice today? I don't know exactly what you need to hear, but I can give a reasonably good guess that

- we need to prepare for the coming of Christ by clearing the clutter out of our hearts and overstuffed lives;
- we need to prepare for the coming of Christ by repentance and restoring of relationships; and
- we need to prepare for the coming of Christ by grabbing hold of a new hope that there is truly a better way of living by following Christ. Amen.

29

Second Sunday of Advent Journey Away from Chaos to Peace

Preparatory Reading: Matthew 11:28

> How restful is your sleep? Or, better yet, how restful is your life? Do you find any peace, or is your life wound so tightly that you are continually agitated and troubled? Can Christ offer us anything in the midst of our burdened lives?
>
> He says he will bring rest to our souls. What's going on here? Is he wrong, or have we failed to allow him into our busy lives? Think about it. Welcome to a time of reflection and meditation.

Prayer: Oh, God, we come before you as a distracted and disturbed people. We are lacking peace. We are lacking rest. We find ourselves accepting the norms of the culture around us, and it isn't working so well for us. Bring us the realization of the rest and peace you offer to us. We pray in the name of Jesus who exhibited and offers peace to us. Amen.

A string walks into a bar. The bartender says, "We don't serve strings here." He crumples him up and tosses him out on to the sidewalk where he gets all scraped up and tangled. The string walks right back in and orders a drink. Amazed, the bartender asks, "Hey, aren't you that same string I just threw out?" The string answers, "No, I'm a frayed knot!"

A "frayed knot" is not too lacking of a description of many of our lives. We pack our bags and get on board a train that is barreling down the tracks and we are hanging on for dear life. Like a cartoon character, our bodies are hanging out the window and we are gripping the side of the supersonic train of busyness and "hurryupness."

We can sing about *Peace Like a River*, and I suppose the author of that song imagined a calm, serene river floating lazily along. But somehow, our river has become a raging torrent, and our peace has slipped out of our grasp and wash somewhere far downstream. Instead of "peace like a river," some of us have turmoil and agitation like a river raging out of control.

In a past issue of *The Family Networker*, there is an article titled "See How They Run: When Did Childhood Turn into a Rat Race?" The article goes on to describe the problem in our culture of childhood becoming "a rat race of hyper scheduling, overbusyness, and loss of family time"[60] and how we are preoccupied with visible signs of success. You know as well as I do that we are not just overscheduling our children—we adults are just as bad.

Who among us has not during the last month made some statement about how busy we are? Where can rest and peace find a place to jump on board in our lives when we do everything we can to exclude them from our lives? If rest and peace were persons, they would be lonely indeed and feel the rejection of a people too focused on their daily planner to acknowledge them.

That is the real issue anyway, isn't it? We can become so hurried and harried that we lose sight of relationships. We don't really have time for each other. And when we do take time to be together, we are not focusing on each other; we are thinking about the next event on our agenda.

If you have driven from Nashville to Chattanooga, you know that you have to go over Monteagle Mountain. The road it extremely steep. As a boy growing up outside of Chattanooga, I remember hearing on the radio of many tractor trailer trucks crashing into that mountain. Finally, they built what they call "runaway truck ramps" so there are ramps to the side of the interstate filled with pebbles to absorb the momentum of any truck that is out of control. They can run up the ramp and safely stop. Do you ever need a life runaway ramp to help us get back on track and absorb the dangerous momentum of your life? At what speed are you traveling?

So where is your peace? Where is your rest? I mean true rest and peace? Maybe these words will be removed from our vocabulary soon for we barely remember what they mean; much less, do we remember the real experience of what they are like?

What do you see when you look in the mirror? I know, I know, some of us see more wrinkles and more receding hairlines and increasing waistlines, but do you ever stop long enough as you rush to get presentable and look at yourself? What is important to the person in the mirror? What does the person in the mirror need?

In our hyperparenting, hyperactive, hyperscheduled, hyperbusy, hypersaturated, hyperdriving, hyper-rushing, and overall hyperburdened lives, what in the world do we need for our troubled souls? Anyone have a troubled soul? Anyone long for peace? Anyone long for rest? Were we not created for more than this?

If you were attempting to slowly erode your life, wouldn't you simply take your focus off what matters and overschedule your life so that you no longer have time for true connecting with other people and connecting with our God? We haven't even mentioned God! Where do we fit God in any of this?

Maybe we can squeeze God in, maybe we can pencil God into our agenda, but make sure you don't write it in ink; there just might be an activity that comes along that will boot him out! Sorry, God, but you will have to be rescheduled. Reschedule God? Sure. God is always available; God can wait. Problem is, we never get around to finding time for God.

Maggie Ross gave a wonderful illustration of seeing a Christmas card with a shepherd on the hillside with his dog when the angels come to announce the birth of Jesus. She tells how she can imagine the shepherd trying to get the dog to quit barking long enough to hear the message. Then she states, "I often wonder if all the fretful, frenetic activity in our lives isn't a human way of barking at angels."[61] She refers to the signs all around us, calling us to pay attention to what matters.

We come to our scripture today realizing that there is something here that calls out to our troubled lives. Our passage calls out to us to slow down and—take note—to notice what really matters. Maybe Christ does have something to offer us after all: rest. Wow! That gets my attention. Doesn't it get yours? And I can surely identify with the writer of Philippians 4:7 when he says that God's peace transcends understanding, as I said we barely even understand the word *peace* any more. It is like a foreign word we have heard before but do not understand.

The first word in Matthew 11:28 may be the most difficult for us, for it says "Come." Jesus says *come* to me. Can we ever find time to do that? The whole passage is, and what it offers is predicated upon having a relationship with Christ. "Come to me," he says. Well, Lord, I plan to get with you a little later. Just give me a minute here. I have to get this done first. And we live our lives with good intentions and continue to plan to get with Christ but fail to do so. But he invites. He says "Come to me."

Notice that he invites "all"—a little word we can all crawl into—"all you who are weary and burdened." He does not specify what kind of weariness or burden it may be. You see, he doesn't want to leave anyone out. He wants all of us to come, no matter what is troubling our souls, no matter what is making us weary. Even if we don't know what is causing our turmoil, he says "Come." And what is he offering? Wow, he is offering rest! Christ offers rest and he offers peace. Look over at John 14: 27: "Peace I leave with you; my peace I give to you."

Anyone need any peace? Anyone need any rest? A kind of rest not based upon external circumstances? Peace that is not dependent upon what is crashing down around us? Christ says, "I will give you rest." Empathically Christ says, no matter how others are treating you, no matter what is happening, I will give you rest! He offers rest to us. He doesn't say we have to earn it and that it is based upon our performance as the religious leaders of his day are saying.

Now, we come to an interesting play of words that seem to be contradictory, but Christ makes them work together. When we think of a yoke or a burden, we think of work and toil. But Christ says in Matthew 11:29–30, "For my yoke is easy and my burden is light." How can he use the term for the tool used to make oxen work in his day and make it sound like something good?

He is being creative with words and taking his yoke is first of all based upon coming to him; and when we yoke with Christ, he is with us in all that we do. He pulls the weight of life. Oh, there remains much for us to do in life as well, but Christ can take a load off us. He gives us rest of soul. In the midst of all kind of external circumstances, Christ can calm our souls. He moves us to see life freshly and clearly in the midst of all that tugs at our coat sleeve.

He doesn't take us out of the world and its problems or even some of it busyness, but he can give us a perspective that changes the way we live in the midst of our busyness. Sometimes, it may mean that we do not let the culture squeeze us into it mold, and at other times he gives us rest in the midst of the craziness of our culture.

His burden is light. How can a burden be light? Contradiction? I think his burden is light because he is carrying most of the load for us. Here, Christ is comparing his way with the way of the people of his day who placed all sorts of unnecessary burdens upon persons for them to do, particularly in their religious walk. It has remained a temptation down through centuries to place unnecessary burdens upon persons when Christ simply says "Come to me." That is his condition, not some performance principle. His is a simple invitation to come into relationship with him.

It is light because of our motive for following him. Motive makes the burden light. This is a weak human example, but it helps me somewhat. To be honest, knowing what I know now, you could not pay me to be a parent! It is just too much of a burden, but on the other hand, could you now pay enough to give up my parenting? No way. It has its difficult moments, but the motive of love for my children makes it much lighter. If I did not love them, it would be an impossibility. Or ask a lover if what she does for her lover is hard or easy. The burden finds another place in the context of love.

When we come to Christ and realize his love for us, life takes on a new perspective. Whatever burden we may carry becomes lighter in the light of his love. The motive of relationship and love make it easy. Are peace and rest even possible in the chaos of our lives today? Or do we simply have to live our lives as frayed knots and ragged edges? May I suggest that we can and maybe should make some changes in the external way we live our lives; however, ultimately, true rest and peace come in relationship with God.

Listen, really listen, to these words of Christ in Matthew 11:28: "Come unto me, all you who are weary and burdened, and I will give you rest." Is it rest and peace you seek? Then seek Christ and truly find rest for your soul this Advent Season. Amen.

30

Third Sunday of Advent Packing Joy into Your Suitcase for the Journey

Preparatory Reading: Lamentations 5:15; Luke 2:8–14; John 15:11

Does Christmas really mean anything positive to you? Is it anything other than a busy time? What emotions are you experiencing at this time of year? Where is the joy of Christmas? Has it vanished into thin air? Think about it. Welcome to a time of meditation and reflection.

Prayer: Oh, God, we are bobbing up and down with our heads just above the water. We have gotten ourselves into an ocean of things to do and places to be and we are about to be swallowed. We need a lifeline. We are existing, but the joy has left our lives. Come this day and help us reach out and grasp the lifeline of Jesus, who is our joy. In his name, we pray. Amen.

How are you doing? Are you surviving okay? How do we get into all this craziness this time of year? It has caused someone to rewrite the words of a familiar Christmas carol, "O Little Town of Bethlehem" has become "O Little Town of Headaches." One day, we could start singing, "O little town of heartaches, how troubled we see thee lie. Throughout thy deep and dream-tossed sleep our fears go marching by. And in thy dark thoughts dwelleth our everlasting fright. The dread and tears of all the years are visiting tonight."

A person's subconscious was apparently working when they had a typo in the church bulletin. The church bulletin declared, "The choir will sing 'I Heard the *Bills* on Christmas Day.'"

Maybe the words of Lamentations have become true of us: "Joy has gone from our hearts our joy has turned to mourning" (Lam. 5:15). At least joy and serenity have turned into bad attitudes and chaos for many.

Amid it all, we have little room for the peace of God and the celebration of Jesus in the manner it should be. I heard of one young girl, upon hearing about that first Christmas night and there being no room at the inn, simply muttered, "It's Joseph's fault. He should have made reservations." She must have been influenced by some things her mother said from time to time about her dad, don't you guess?

Maybe our failure to celebrate the Jesus part of Christmas is because we have failed to make reservations with God and pull aside for a little while to experience the magnitude of the gift of Jesus. Bowed over with the weight of a truckload of cares, we sometimes stagger and bruise our knees on the journey of life, especially this time of year. Like a vacuum cleaner sucking up a valuable coin, we experience life pulling and tugging the positive energy right out of our souls. There are times when we lose the capacity to experience this wonderful feeling we call joy.

The Bible says, "What has happened to all your joy?" (Gal. 4:15). Persons were once excited about Jesus and now had gotten focused on other things. And what a question it is for you and me as well: "What has happened to all your joy?" Wow, it hits home, does it not? What has happened to your joy?

Think about these thoughts for a while:

- The children look at us and wonder if we are excited about Jesus or if we have become Scrooge. Which do we most emulate?
- We speak of the peace of Christ while we are yelling at each other because of the stress level we are under.
- We have somehow taught our children to want everything they see so they are never satisfied but for fleeting moments and we wonder what we have taught them about the contentment of Jesus.
- We fill our moments to the bursting point, and then we wonder why we get frustrated with the season.

What has happened to our joy? Reminds me of those words from Dante's *Inferno*:

> In the middle of the journey of our life
> I found myself in a dark wood,
> For I had lost the right path.[62]

To paraphrase,

> In the middle of the Christmas season
> We have found ourselves in a dark mood
> For we have lost our joy about Jesus.

Maybe we should become like the Committee to Save Merry Christmas some time ago that has charged Macy's with trying to remove Christmas from Christmas. The committee to save Merry Christmas announced a national boycott against Macy's and Federated Department Stores for the 2004 season.[63]

Maybe we should seek to force people to be joyous during this season. We could pass laws so that all those walking along the sidewalk or in the stores or even in the churches that do not have an expression of joy on their faces be arrested or have to pay a fine. There might be more arrests in our churches than on our city streets, don't you think? There are some who want to legislate everything and would probably love something like this.

Of course, I am being facetious and I agree with Don Evans who wrote this about the boycott against Macy's:

> What makes all of this silly, of course, is the idea that forcing a retailer to restore the phrase "Merry Christmas" to its marketing strategy somehow promotes Christianity. What it actually does is make Christians look like bullies who don't seem to care that we share the country with people of other faiths.[64]

Trying to force persons to be joyous would be a form of bullying as well and simply would not work. There are things that we do not legislate or force from the outside; they must come from within the heart.

As Jesus told his disciples in the passage from John 15:11 that he came so that our joy might be complete. Jesus is a means to finding more joy in life. The Christian concept of joy includes gladness, celebration, and a deep happiness.

What has happened to our joy? Do we need any joy or gladness or true celebration or deep happiness in our lives? There was a little package, a little bundle of joy, who came wrapped in human flesh some two thousand years ago.

Most of us are afraid to hold the package. We are afraid we might get too attached. We are afraid we might be changed or challenged or transformed. We prefer to remain at a distance and observe the child from afar. We dare not unwrap this package. It might be too much for us. And we have developed all kinds of nice-sounding stories and manger scenes and wise men and songs, and we have removed the very power of the words that this package taught us when it was unwrapped.

What has happened to our joy? Joy has to do with attitude, and it goes beyond or overcomes the circumstances of life. It does not just always happen; it is a way of approaching life. Well, we have been so much at taming his coming and his teaching that we have shut out how fantastic they really are.

When we shut down whole chunks of ourselves to survive, we substitute all kinds of ineffective toys to take the place of our real selves. We ignore God, and so we make our own little commercial gods that lay all kinds of burdens upon us. What has happened to our joy? We have failed to really receive him and celebrate him and all he stands for and we have, therefore, missed his joy.

Can you begin to find room for him this Christmas? Can you begin to receive him this Christmas? Can you begin to welcome him into your heart this Christmas? Can you begin to celebrate him this Christmas?

Later in his writing that I quoted earlier, Dante comes to a more hopeful point and writes, "And so we came forth, and once again beheld the stars."[65] May we come forth this Christmas and once again behold Jesus. In finding him, we will also find joy. Amen.

31

Fourth Sunday of Advent The Return to What Matters—Love

Preparatory Reading: Matt. 13:1–12

> Is there any place of beginning again in your life? Is there any place you can point to and say "My life changed for the better on that day"? How far away are you from that place of beginning again? Would it be good to somehow in some manner return to that place of beginning again? The message God gives to us is, you can begin again! Think about it. Welcome to a time of meditation and reflection.

Prayer: Oh, God, during this wonderful season of Advent, we ask that you might help us to center our lives around you instead of around so many things that keep us from you. We ask that we might return to fully knowing and experiencing you and your grace in our lives. For we pray in the spirit of the babe of Bethlehem. Amen.

The story goes that Joe had asked Bob to help him out with the deck after work, so Bob just went straight over to Joe's place. When they got to the door, Joe went straight to his wife, gave her a hug, and told her how beautiful she was and how much he had missed her at work. She was happy for his return home. When it was time for supper, he complimented his wife on her cooking, kissed her, and told her how much he loved her.

Once they were working on the deck, Bob told Joe that he was surprised that he fussed so much over his wife. Joe said that he'd started this about six months prior and it had revived their marriage and things couldn't be better. Bob thought he'd give it a go.

When Bob got home, he gave his wife a massive hug, kissed her, and told her that he loved her. His wife burst into tears! Bob was confused and asked why she was crying. She said, "This is the worst day of my life. First, little Billy fell off his bike and twisted his ankle. Then, the washing machine broke and flooded the basement. And now, you come home drunk!"

We sometimes take returning home for granted. We often resume our contact without any real fanfare. It is just routine and habitual, so we do not want to make a fuss every time we return. It is nice to have some kind of greeting when we meet, such as a hug or kiss, that becomes at least a routine symbol of our reuniting with our spouses. However, that being said, at times, I think maybe we should be encouraged to make returning more special with flowers or some other way to show that we are happy for a person's return or our return to meet them.

What about returns when the absence has been longer? Do you recall times of returning in your life? Returns can have powerfully important meanings for us. They can be times of reacquaintance and restoring of relationships. We think of people returning. Some of you returned from a long time away. Maybe you were in a branch of the military and did service away or served in a war. What was it like to return home? How much anticipating did you do?

Maybe you went away to school or college. How did it feel to come home, to come back? Maybe some of you even ran away from home in your youth. How did it feel to come back home? Maybe some of you moved away from friends and family at some point. How was it coming home? How was it getting reacquainted?

Some of you went to class reunions? How was it to return to see all the people that seemed so much older than you? Maybe you worked out of town for an extended period of time. How was your anticipation of returning home?

How is it to return in a good sense? One author encouraged readers to "refuse to live yesterday over and over again."[66] That can be such great counsel, but there are times when we need to return to places of meaning and purpose in our lives. There are times when we have traveled far from that which gave us life and health in our lives. Probably one of the best known of stories about such is the story of that is called the prodigal son in the gospel of Luke. The son leaves his father and travels into a far county and it literally breaks his father's heart. The son gets lost in wild and senseless living in the faraway land, and his move has included traveling far away from that which gave meaning and purpose to his life.

Finally, as you know, he has a desperate return home to find himself again and to restore his spiritual life and his sanity. It is a grand return for his father who celebrates lavishly in his great joy over his son's return. It is a grand old love story of how God loves and accepts each of us.

We do not need to return to our bad times in life and the times of destruction, but there can be times when we need to return to times of meaning. There are times we need to go back to the beginning of the fork in the road that led us in the wrong direction, and we need to begin again and take the other fork in the road.

Here we are on this Sunday of Advent, and we have this strange biblical text about strange John the Baptist. But maybe it is appropriate to have his text at this time, for Advent is a time of preparation, a time of preparation for the coming of the Christ Child. We are to get ready, we are to wake up, we are to come out of hiding, and we are to find God.

Let's remind ourselves again of what we discussed in an earlier chapter. We will briefly look again at the call to repentance. John the Baptist shouted, "Repent for the Kingdom of Heaven is near" (Matt. 3:2). Frederick Buechner defined repentance this way: "To repent is to come to your senses."[67] Wow!

That can resonate with us if we will allow it to, can it not? That time in our lives is to be a time when we come to our senses. We need to reflect during this time and realize what is important in and for our lives, and we need to wake up and come to our senses and get on track.

Sometimes when you wake up in the morning, you may do some stupid things as you are not fully present and you are not fully alert while awaking. Maybe the call here is, saying, "You are going through life not fully present or fully awake." Come to your senses and see what really matters in life and move toward it!

Marcus Borg wrote about repentance as a "return" or "resolve" and meaning to "reconnect with God," and he shows that in the Christian scriptures that the Greek root means "to go beyond the mind that you have." He makes the case for repentance truly implying change.[68] So this Advent Season, we are being called to come to our senses, to return to life in God, and to move beyond the staleness in which we may find ourselves.

This season can be a wonderful time. It is to be a wonderful time of returning in a positive sense to the God who gives meaning and purpose to living. It is a time to reflect and to consider how we need to come back to God, to return to his favor, to return to the fullness of life in God.

Do you somehow need to return to a life centered in God? Do you somehow need to return from a far country where God has been absent? Do you need to wake up and come to your senses about the important issues of life and return to having such priorities in your life? Barbara Brown Taylor put it well: "Do not put off living the kind of life you meant to live."[69]

It is easy, ever so easy, during the year to gradually and ever so slowly move away from the things that matter. We have so many demands placed upon us. We have so much calling for our attention. We have so little time to meditate and reflect upon the direction of our lives. Please don't put off too long what really matters. Amen.

32

The Longest Night Service
Moving from Nope to Hope

Preparatory Reading: Psalm 51:10–12

The original version of this chapter was presented when I was a guest speaker at First United Methodist Church of Rome for their longest night service. Therefore, I had to be clear with my members from First Christian (Disciples of Christ) of Rome, where I was senior minister at the time, that the longest night service was because of the length of the night and not because it just seems like the longest night because I am speaking!

Jesus once said "A prophet is without honor in his own country," and it is also true that a preacher is without honor in his own church, so I was attempting to head off the ribbing I would get about the longest night deal. It didn't work, and they gave me a difficult time anyway! Actually, they treated me very well, however, and we had a lot of good-natured give-and-take.

Prayer: Oh, God, slow us down for we have been in a hurry to nowhere special. We are running, running, fleeing from our fears and failures and the hard knocks of life. Slow us down and come with your spirit of peace to heal us and give us hope we pray in the spirit of the Christ who revealed better how to walk with you. Amen.

F. Scott Fitzgerald, as you may know, was one of America's most admired authors in the 1920s, but he described himself as being like a cracked plate. By the 1930s, his life had been through great upheaval, and he experienced great despair. In a series of articles in *Esquire* magazine, he was candid about how empty his life had become and the morass in which he found himself. In a very powerful manner, he wrote of his despair saying, "In a real dark night of the soul, it is always 3 o'clock in the morning—day after day."[70]

There are times in our lives when the night is oh so very long and oh so very dark and when our soul groans a million groans of anguish, trembling agony, and utter despair. During such times, it does feel like it is always 3:00 a.m. Can you admit to such times? A part of us would like to deny such and not mention them. Especially around the Christmas holidays, we do not especially wish to think of those who are having tough times, if our lives are going pretty well at the time. However, tonight, we pause and consider how difficult life is for some and that some are having a very long night on this longest night of the year. We also acknowledge our own times of difficulty in life.

Therefore, tonight, I want us to face head on the reality that life is not always fair and that life can have some very hard and difficult places. We do not cope best, I do not believe, by denial and putting our heads in the sand or by some phony and empty Pollyanna religious talk. And if we surround ourselves in some pseudoholy cloth of escapism, how then do we minister to troubled souls? We must not deny the fact we all have troubles in life!

Truth is, sorrow comes walking up all our sidewalks and knocks at all our doors. If it has not happened to you yet, mark my word, it will. There are times when sorrow does not even knock and instead intrudes boldly and rudely right into our personal spaces.

Darkness closes in around us, and the child of winter penetrates our soul. Scholar Martin Marty once wrote, "Winter is a season of the heart as it is a season of the weather."[71] So we come together for this longest night service, recognizing that in the midst of the holidays, right smack dab in among the Christmas trees and cheer and the manger scenes and Christmas cookies, this may very well be a time when all the hard knocks of the year come back with the force of a blizzard to chill our souls to the core.

Events may have happened during the year that make us feel like we are sliding down a hill on black ice. If you have ever slid on ice in your car, you can identify with that, can you not? However, when it is your life spinning out of control, it may be even more terrifying than a car spinning out of control.

Hard times, bad times, sad times, loss and rejection, abandonment and loneliness, relationship breakups, financial devastations, illness and disease, verbal and physical attacks, letting go of loved ones, and on and on we could go. The shadows fall and the darkness overcomes. We can identify with psalmist and cry out with him: "For troubles without number surround me" (Ps. 40:12). It all is enough to make us agree with the philosophers that "life is an endless pain with a painful end."[72]

Life may have brought its cold chill to your heart this year. Life may have said "No, nope, no way, no deal." Life may have brought your progress to a halt, a stopping point. It may have poured negativity into your spirit like rain flowing down a drain spout. Life may have snatched your hope away like a leaf torn from a tree in a fierce storm. And it hurts; it hurts profoundly and deeply.

So, is this where we have come to on this longest night? Do we just sit down and freeze to death in the gloom and darkness of this bleak winter of the soul? Do we give in to the dampness and the blackness of life?

I trust that, with me, you will shout "No!" We have to come to hope against hope and hope, especially hope against nope. The "nopes" of life cannot win. The nos of life will not win. They will not win. I believe that there is something in evil and negativity and badness that will eventually cause it to crash of its own accord. And I also believe there is something in the human spirit, there is something in the spirit we have from God what is born over and over again out of the bleakest of moments.

Just as the daffodil raises it head in the cold winter, so does the human spirit. In the darkest night, the star shines brightest. And even during the longest night, the sun begins to dawn. To paraphrase Psalm 30:5, weeping and tossing and turning may clutch my soul all night long. but joy relieves me in the morning! Our hope is that relief finally arrives. Help eventually comes. We have a God of healing and hope! This is our faith—cling to it.

It is written in the scheme of things, and the biblical themes bring it forth: Out of chaos, there is creation; out of death, there is resurrection; in the darkness, a light appears; in the midst of brokenness, there is new life; in the midst of a crooked way, there is made a straight path; after winter, spring follows; and in the midst of a self-destructing world, there is a new earth. Bad times do not last forever. This is our faith. This is our faith.

A great thing about our belief in God is that it helps us to see that everything is not as it appears at the moment. There is a God behind the scenes seeking to work for our good, bringing healing and bringing the cycle of good back around.

The Good News is that during those times, when we are speechless because of the tragedies of life, God hears our groans and not only hears them but understands them. Even in the deepest nights of the soul, when we feel our hearts are breaking in two, when sleep eludes us at 3:00 a.m., and even when we are hurting so badly that words fail us, there is a God who can be reached by our groans and who will hear us. In 2 Corinthians 4:9, Paul writes, "We are hard pressed on every side, but not crushed, perplexed but not in despair, persecuted but not abandoned, struck down but not destroyed." Wow! What a truth but also what an encouragement! This is our faith.

Life does not always go as it should, but the Christian endures by knowing that God truly hears our deepest pain and is in our pain with us. In the chaos and confusion of the profound hurts of long and dark nights, this is the good news that comes to us, and we must to cling to at all times. No matter how dark it may seem or how cold the chill of life may become, I believe God loves us still! Always remember, when life says "Nope!" God says "Hope!" When life says "No deal," God says "I will help you heal!" This is our faith, this is our faith—cling to it! Amen.

33

Christmas Eve Following the Light

Preparatory Reading: John 1:1–9

Are you afraid of the dark? Things can get a bit spooky in the darkness. Life can seem worse in the darkness. Sometimes in life, we are surrounded by darkness and afraid. Think about it. Welcome to a time of meditation and reflection.

Prayer: Oh, God, into our darkness of soul, come and shed your wonderful light and warmth. In the name of the one who was a bright and shining star. Amen.

We still use this analogy: When I say that "I was in the dark about it." You know what I mean, don't you? Of course, it means "I did not know about it." *Darkness, in the dark, in the shadows*—any hint of darkness has a hint of fear and uncertainly in it. Darkness is sometimes like a freight train bearing down on a compact car; it is frightening. Sometimes, it is like bone-chilling wetness that presses against our skin like old clothing after a storm. Darkness haunts us. Darkness chases us. Darkness surrounds us. We all have our own dark shadows lurking after us.

Making decisions in the dark can lead to some regrettable consequences. Don't ever buy a car at night. Don't attempt to walk through the house at night in the darkness. Back in the days before electricity, a tightfisted old farmer was taking his hired man to task for carrying a lit lantern when he went to call on his best girl. "Why," he exclaimed, "when I went a-courtin' I never carried one of them things. I always went in the dark."

"Yes," the hired man quipped," and look what you got!"

Some are against progress and remain in the dark, and it has consequences. In some ways, it seems humankind chooses some darkness. Some choose more darkness than others. But ultimately, darkness is a symbol of the unlimited horizons of badness and sinfulness.

However, light has a different connotation. Light shows the way. It illumines the pathway. Light gives us direction. Light gives us warning. Light gives us hope.

At the time of Christ's birth, many were, as today, groping about in the darkness and confusion of the madness of their world. There was uncertainty, poverty, strife, class struggles, and pain. There was loneliness, abandonment, and rejection. There was mistreatment, maltreatment, wickedness, and sinfulness. Humans have always had such ingredients aplenty. Even early on, it was so.

But into the great darkness stepped a God with a promise, a God who made a promise of one who would be the light of the world. Into the darkness danced a God who had Christmas in his heart. In absolute darkness, light blinds so the light could be at first only dimly understood. The light could only carefully be revealed. The light came in the face of a child so that it would grow and gradually reveal God's glory.

The authors of the gospels use fireworks of angels exploding into the darkness to announce the coming of the light. The God who, in the beginning, tried to get things going in the right direction by saying "Let there be light" (Gen. 1:3); now in essence, announces again, "Let there be light and let it be found in the small form of a baby and grow in it revelation of brightness and brilliance."

There is much around the Christmas story to suggest that Jesus is light—the brightness of a hillside of angels, the star to be followed—and then Jesus is called the light of the world. Those who find the Christ of Christmas are "the people living in darkness have seen a great light," according to Matthew 4:16 as he quotes Isaiah. The babe born in Bethlehem is the promise of God in the darkness; he is God dancing into the darkness. He ever shines more brightly if we will allow him, my friends. Christ is the light that can shine in the darkest moments of our lives. His face is there behind any and every cloud of darkness, shining with the light of his great love and care for us.

Is he but faintly shining in your heart? Wouldn't you like for him to be born anew in the stable or cradle of your heart tonight? Will you make room for him? Will you allow him to dispel the darkness? And you know what, he wants you to be his reflection in this dark world. He wants his light to shine through you and me. He is a bright face in the darkness of the world, and he wants us to be his face to those around us.

The question for us this Christmas Eve is this—and is it a very important question—Will we allow the darkness to overcome the world, or will we allow him to be the God of a thousand faces (our faces) glowing in the world and overcoming the darkness by his grace?

Light or darkness is set before us this day. May we choose the light. May we choose the Christ of Christmas! Amen.

Prayer: Oh, God, the Advent wreath is now fully lit because we celebrate the coming of Christ. And we pray that you who are the light of the world may come and shine in our faces this day is our prayer. Amen.

34

Christmas Let's Cancel Christmas ... or Should We?

Preparatory Reading: Luke 2:1–14; Colossians 2:16–23

Did you notice my chapter title, "Let's Cancel Christmas ... or Should We?" I really wanted it to be just simply "Let's Cancel Christmas!" but I didn't have the guts to leave it like that. I was afraid some of you might throw this book in the trash. Therefore, I added "or Should We?"

What about this season we are entering? Does it have any meaning for you anymore? I wonder whether we might somehow discover or rediscover more meaning in Christmas this year. It is my hope that this will be a special season for us. Think about it. Welcome to a time of meditation and reflection.

Prayer: Oh, God, as we start down that old familiar pathway to the manger scene, may we find something new in the well-worn but little-realized story of the Good News that came wrapped in swaddling clothes. Amen.

Someone in our family—I shall not reveal who—at times has gotten up at 5:00 a.m. on Black Friday morning so she could get to the stores by the time they were open at 6:00 a.m. for Christmas Shopping. Now, I am an early riser, but you will not find me getting up at that hour for that purpose. I understand—although, of course, I have not experienced it—that the crowds are like cattle crowding through the gate at feeding time. Or maybe we should say like cattle being led to slaughter?

They are like bees swarming around their hive, and if you don't watch out, some person, "in the Christmas Spirit," will sting you if you accidentally bump into or pick up an item they want. We have all heard the bizarre stories of persons getting in fights while trying to buy that last toy for their child so the child can experience the joy of Christmas. Something doesn't quite fit about that.

What about this holiday time? Should we just cancel it and go on about our business? I mean, some travel hundreds of miles to be with persons they really don't like and receive gifts they really, really don't want.

And the food. We all plan to go on a diet at the first of the year. We know it is impossible to avoid eating too much in that time from Thanksgiving to Christmas.

The busyness is unreal. Our schedules get packed like a worn-out suitcase bursting at the seams. There is not a moment to spare—gifts to buy, food to prepare, decorations to hang (how can those Christmas tree light get so tangled in storage?) cards to send, parties to attend, travel to endure. We begin to long for one, single, solitary "Silent Night" or wish we could go away to the hillside with the shepherds of long ago. Someone said of this time, "Away in a manger, I wish I were there!"

Do we really want to do all this? We have romanticized this time as the time when families and friends get along perfectly. Everyone is supposedly happy and friendly and all smiles. Songs are idealistic, and TV commercials show only holiday cheer. (Although one store had one that is more realistic: A woman is sitting, saying something like "Twelve boxes of chocolates and a bunch of knickknacks that I don't need. You know what I really need is some underpants!")

However, most presentations are very idealistic. The truth is, we all know quite well that this time of the year is also a very difficult time for many people. In fact, it is rather painful as we wrote about in a previous chapter.

Our family had a personal horrific tragedy and loss on Christmas day years ago. There is a certain sadness for us at this time. Many who have lost loved ones feel the loss acutely during the holidays. Those who are alone or who have an illness may struggle through the season with many tears and fears. We do have the term *holiday blues* that describes some sense of this downside of the holidays.

So maybe we should just cancel this whole thing and save our Tums and Rolaids. It would certainly not give such a yearly death-blow to our budgets. We would have time available to watch more football games, and what could be better than that?

Let's cancel Christmas. Let's just cancel Christmas. What do you think? We could just skip over that holiday. In fact, the writings of Paul's epistles are earlier than the gospels, and he or the authors of the epistles do not make not a big deal about the birth of Christ. We could theologically base our decision to cancel Christmas on the approach Paul takes and even be biblically justified in during so. Some say that the gospel writers embellished the story with things that really did not happen. Some remind us that Christ was really born in the spring anyway, and December 25 is based on a pagan holiday, and there is some truth to that. Let's just cancel Christmas.

Why do you really celebrate Christmas? I mean, it rolls around each year, but why do we really celebrate? Does it have any meaning any more, or is it just a tradition, a ritual with no real purpose in our lives?

Let cancel Christmas ... or should we? Some readers are probably shouting "Amen" internally—and you would really like to cancel Christmas. Perhaps, for most, hopefully, I have stirred just a bit of rebuttal in you, and you are ready to defend at least part of the reason for celebrating this season. But maybe we do need to pause and look at it anew.

We will not do a full study of the scripture for this chapter in Colossians 2:16–25. However, it does remind us that the church was faced with those who sought impose an overabundance of "do nots" in the church. "Do not do this," "Do not taste eat this or drink that" (and for healthful living, there is some merit in moderation of many things, yet these are not requirements for us), "Do not touch that," "Do not, do not, do not." I am sure today they would love a sermon entitled, "Let's Cancel Christmas." But note what Paul wrote in Colossians 2:23. A religion based on don'ts and on not doing external behaviors is a false religion and doesn't even work anyway.

There is an wonderful old story that is now somewhat worn out but still a useful story of men working in a marble mine, and it goes something like this: A person meets one of the men working in the mine and asks him what he is doing. He replies, "What does it look like I am doing? I am working my hands to the bone working in this mine." The person meets a second person working at the mine and asks him what he is doing. He replies, "Oh, I am working to provide for my wonderful family. This work provides for my family." The person goes on and meets a third worker and again asks the question, what are you doing? This worker replies, "Oh, I am helping to prepare a magnificent cathedral where people from all lands will come and be inspired by its beauty."

Let's cancel Christmas. Let cancel it, in the sense that it is just another year of busyness and a headache to be endured. Let's cancel Christmas, in the sense that it is something to be denied and avoided because of our fear of excess. Let's cancel Christmas, in terms of a myopic focus on excessive commercialism.

But, oh, my friends, let us celebrate Christmas where we see the larger picture and experience the majesty and awe of it all. However we interpret or understand the birth of Christ, the world is not the same because of his birth. Could we somehow allow God to break into our lives as he did for those on that Christmas morning so long ago?

There is majesty here. There is glory here. It will move all around us again this Christmas despite all the imperfections of our world and of our celebrating, but if we are not careful we will miss it and go on about our business and busyness and never be changed by his presence. God can break through it all. Can we pause long enough today to see the majesty of it?

Peter Marshall, who had a much better title for a Christmas sermon than mine—"Let's Keep Christmas"—said these words in that sermon:

> Let's not permit the crowds and the rush to crowd Christmas out of our hearts ... for that is where it belongs. Christmas is not in the stores—but in the hearts of people."[73]

Christmas is here. Shall we not celebrate? Jesus desires to come into our hearts this Christmas. No, let's not cancel Christmas. Let's celebrate it like never before and with a sense of its majesty and splendor and magnificence and wonder and amazement and bewilderment and astonishment. Let's eat and drink and have fun. Let's enjoy each other and the precious moments we share together. Let's overflow—to use the term of our scripture, overflow—with thanksgivings. Let's enjoy the songs of Christmas. Let's laugh and be joyous and happy, and let us this Christmas catch a glimpse of the wonderful God we serve. After all, it is the Christmas!

CLOSING OUT OLD YEAR

This is not one of the holy days of the Christian Year, although some have special services on New Year's Eve to end the year. It seems appropriate to have some reflection on closing out the year and the past. There are things we need to let go of and things we need to carry with us as we prepare to transition to a new year.

The Closing of the Old Year

35

It Is Time to Let Go of the Past and Move Forward!

Preparatory Reading: Philippians 3:1–13

The little boy was being taught about reverence in church by his Sunday school teacher. "And Johnny why are we very quiet during the church service?" the teacher asked.

"Because everyone is sleeping!" Johnny replied.

Some of us sleep in church, others of us sleep through life, but by sleeping we may miss something. Sometimes, in the normal course of events, something happens. And believe it or not, sometimes—occasionally—something special, something out of the ordinary, could even happen as the year closes and a new one begins.

Actually, it could be that God might speak to you—that is, if you are not sleeping and you are listening for God's voice. It might just be some good news about yourself that you will miss reading. So, I encourage you to stay alert. Something could transform a life. It could be yours. Think about it. Welcome to a time of reflection and meditation.

Prayer: Oh, God, we try to find spiritual nourishment in so many false places. We even seek to live off past mistakes

*and failures and think that we can find sustenance there,
but it does not work. Bring us back to you and the vision
and vitality you bring into our lives is our prayer in the spirit
of Jesus. Amen.*

I recall reading a story told by a minister, and I want to use and adapt just one part of it this morning: He was a visiting preacher, and a woman came up to him before the service and said to him, "I need to know something." And he said, "Yes ma'am." She said, "Before I listen to you, I need to ask. Are you a knocked-down, killed-in-the-Spirit, washed-clean, picked-up, Spirit-filled, charismatic, '*dunked under the water,' hellfire-condemning, rapture-waiting, snake-handling, pew-jumping* Christian?[74]" Well, I added the part about "dunked under the water, hellfire-condemning, rapture-waiting, snake-handling, and pew-jumping"; but you get the picture!

This lady had a list of things to which you had to line up or she did not consider you a real, genuine Christian or maybe a Christian at all. Before we chuckle too much, maybe we should ask ourselves if we do the same as this woman but just not so blatantly. Do we set up judgments as to what a person has to do to be a Christian?

That is one of the reasons the founders of some churches in wisdom established the practice of asking only one question to those desiring to join the church—Are you desiring to and making a commitment to follow Jesus? Otherwise, we get all our personal opinions and beliefs in the way and set up barriers to those who desire to come to God or to the church. But what barriers or obstacles would you set up to those wanting to come to God or join the church if you had your way?

Sometimes, we want godliness measured. We want to be able to look and see how godly someone is. If only they had certain metals or they wore or stripes on their sleeves or pins on their chests that revealed how godly they were, then we would know. If we only knew how close they were to our own theology, that might help for most of us judge others by our own standards. Now, I do think godliness is evident often in persons, but we do not always know. However, many of us would like to simplify it so that we know who is godly and who isn't. Some even want or have a checklist.

I realized how judgmental I can be by a revelation of my daughter years ago. We had a new baseball stadium at the time, and we went to our first Rome Braves ballgame. As we approached the entrance to the ball field, there was a gentleman there on the corner of the street with a large sign and the words "Whosoever believes on the name of the Lord will be saved."

My first reaction was negative, and I mumbled something underneath my breath about him being ridiculous out there while people were trying to go the ballgame and mumbled—in my self-righteousness—how such approaches do more harm to the name of Christ than help. I started to explain to my children how some people go to extremes. But Anna, a ten-year-old, had a much more Christian reaction, and it was quite different from mine.

Anna, in childhood loveliness, when she saw the man with the sign, said, "That's so sweet." And after my little critical explanation of what I thought about what he was doing, Anna said, "At least people know he is a Christian." And I wanted to get into the stadium as fast as I could and crawl under the bleachers in shame. The children teach us.

If we had been in Philippi during the days of Paul, some of us would have been tempted to join another group and some might have left us and went over to join them. They were Gentiles, like the Philippians, but who had also been converted to Judaism and who had a list of things one must do to be a real Christian. They were zealous for their cause. They promoted the law, and they preached the ritual of circumcision, which was an identity mark to the males of Judaism.

They made things black and white and much clearer. Either you were among them and followed certain behaviors or you were outside the fold. It made it easier. And some would love for it to be that way in the church. How about you? How do you desire it to be?

Paul is not so happy about such an approach. He calls such people dogs and mutilates of the flesh. That's pretty strong language. You see, Paul realized that this kind of approach would have destroyed Christianity! It would have destroyed it because it does away with faith in Jesus and puts faith in works; will do and does the same today.

Therefore, to paraphrase what Paul states in Philippians 3:4–6, he says, "Hey, do you want to play that game? I can beat you at it. I have more metals than you do. I have more behaviors that you are requiring than you do." This is the problem with legalist righteousness; it leads to comparisons and "one-upsmanships." However, Paul is using his credentials here to combat a heresy that threatened the church. He could claim all sorts of the credentials of a legalistic approach—he had been there.

But the important verses are Philippians 3:7–8. Once Paul came to Jesus, he saw how spiritually bankrupt such a way of living really is. He had been a star in his circles of legalism. But then he saw how all that was what is politely translated as the word "rubbish." It was a failed religious approach—a bankrupt religious experience, an empty religious practice. It had its focus in all the wrong places. It was rubbish or actually something even smellier if we translated it more literally. Yet churches often continue to find ways to institute legalistic barriers.

Why was this so? How did he know the difference now? Because he had come to know Christ is what verse 8 states. But I must hasten on to another point I want to underscore. If we remember for a moment, we know that Paul had regrets about his legalistic past. Remember, it tells us in Acts that he was present at the stoning, the killing of Stephen, and he at the least held his coat while others stoned him.

Paul must have had regrets about spending so much energy in a bankrupt way of looking at religion and in all the persecution of the earlier Christians that he participated in. He had done some awful things, even in the name of religion. Paul must have had many, many regrets and guilt over what he had done—regrets about all he had missed in his former life, mistakes he had made. But he moved forward with a positive focus. That is why he wrote in Philippians 3:13, "Forgetting what is behind and straining to what lies ahead."

Some years ago, my loving wife and wonderful children talked me into it. I really did not think it was such a great idea, but my family overruled. Therefore, at the beginning of the summer, I went down to Sam's Discount Warehouse and purchased a swimming pool. It was called an "easy setup" pool. That should have been the first clue. Easy setup—yeah right!

It was folded in just the right way to get it into the box in which it came. Do you realize how many millions of dollars the experts that package products save in shipping? I mean, they have it down to a fine science where they can pack something huge into a relatively small box.

Yes, it was an "easy setup pool." Indeed, it was an easy setup all right, a setup for me to lose my religion! Actually, it would have set up fairly easily if you had a perfectly level spot to put it. The easy setup pool holds about 3,000 gallons of water; and if you do not have a level spot when you get to around 2,999 gallons, all of a sudden, the water spills over the lowest point and it is like a great flood as the water begins to push down the side and rush over the wall of the pool—you can lose a kid in such a flood!

One can certainly get the installer soaked! Perhaps, it didn't hold 3,000 gallons of water—that was an estimate—but it surely seemed like it when it pushed me down and along the yard! I had not wanted to buy the thing anyway, and we will not go into how I reminded my family of that or the impact the pool had on my religious experience. Finally, after much trial and tribulation, we got the "easy setup" pool set up.

All too quickly, the end of the summer came, and it was time to take the pool down. I had saved the box it came in. However, I found that the experts at packing are not any friends of mine, and there was no way I could get the pool back into the box.

There is more to this story, but it is not so relevant to our purposes, like the fact that our potbelly pig tore a hole in the side of the pool. So I thought we might get to throw the blame thing away the next year (I mean throw away the pool, not the pig, although that might have been a good idea as well!) However, somehow, many things we purchase will not go back into the box once we take them out. I am sure you have had that experience with some product. And the year is like that—we cannot put back what we have taken out this year. We cannot repackage and send our regrets back. Therefore, we have to find a way forward. The Christian concept of forgiveness is a great means for that. And while on the subject of forgiveness, God, please forgive me for the reaction I had to the easy setup pool!

Seriously, do you have any regrets about your life? I suggest you cannot live too long in this world without building up some regrets. Some are small like my reaction to the pool; others are profound and greatly disturb us. There are things we wish we had done or had not done—opportunities that were lost. We wish things had been different or we had done differently. Do you have any regrets over the year that is ending?

What I want to suggest to us today is that we not allow our regrets in life to bankrupt our todays by paying interest on the regrets of yesterday. Some live on regrets and end up being emotionally weak and famished and anorexic and not able to enjoy life. Some people continually beat themselves up over something or some things they did in the past. Regrets become their daily food, and they are starving themselves emotionally and spiritually.

Regrets do not make good sustenance. They are empty calories that do not nourish our souls. Do you have regrets from this year? Do you have regrets from past years? How much are you trying to live a life on regrets? "I was not a good parent. I was not a good mate, I failed at this or that, I did that wrongly, I blew that one, I missed that opportunity, if only, if only"—do you see how it paralyzes you and keeps you wound up in the past, living with disappointment?

There is a proverb that goes this way: "A person is not old until regrets take the place of their dreams." However, for some of us, that has happened. Regrets replace dreams and make life most miserable.

Paul could have done this to himself. He could have not only been the one with the most credentials in legalistic righteousness, he could have been the one with the biggest regrets and consumed with his regrets; however, he found a way forward with God.

In forgetting the past, some of us are yet weighted down with past mistakes and missteps. Some of us have, therefore, become pessimists. Someone wrote that a pessimist is a person who can hardly wait for the future so he can look back with regret! Is that you?

Allow me to drive this point home even more to the point in some way (as I did in an earlier chapter). Is your church living with past regrets? Is your religious institution saying "If only, if only"—"If only we had some children present", "If only we had more money," "If only we had more members," "If only we had made this decision or that decision years ago"? Is your church living with regrets? Are we looking to the future as pessimists and can hardly wait until then so we can look back with regret about this time in your church history?

Are we trying to live as Christians on regrets or the malnourishment of missed opportunities? If so, it impacts our present vision. Are we saying "We cannot do that, we are too small; we cannot do that, we are too old; we cannot do that, we could never have the money"? On and on the negatives can go. We can start living with so much caution and fear because of our regrets that faith gets tossed out the window.

I read that words were hung on the wall at General Motors—at least, in the past they were there (I don't know about today):

> According to the theory of aerodynamics, and as can be readily proven in wind tunnel experiments, the Bumble Bee is unable to fly. This is because the size of its wings in relation to the size of its body makes flying impossible. But the Bumble Bee, being unacquainted

with these scientific truths goes ahead and flies anyway and gathers a little honey every day.

Maybe, just maybe, as individuals or as churches we need to forget about the past and forget about our regrets and forget about our *"if onlies,"* we need to really focus instead on getting to know God. We need to see the good things God is doing in our midst even now! The coming New Year will provide new opportunities to move in new directions. Let us prepare for it!

For, you see, God does not always work in ordinary ways. Sometimes God appears to be a bit unorthodox. Sometimes God takes a person like the apostle Paul and turns him into a grand influence for his cause. Sometimes God takes a church that is not so big—that does not have so much money, that has made some mistakes in the past—and uses it to do great things in its neck of the woods.

I believe Paul is pointing out that the key to overcome all the weights of the past and even the present is by seeking spiritual realities and relationships. It is time for us to let go of past regrets and move forward as we turn the page into a new year.

And I dare say that if we, as individuals, follow his words in the last part of Philippians 3:13, we will find our vision and our motivation again and not be blinded by our regrets. Note his words again: "Forgetting what is behind and straining toward what is ahead, I press on toward the goal to win the prize for which God has called me heavenward in Christ Jesus."

Let us say *no* to living on the emptiness of past regrets and choose instead to move to greater heights spiritually. Let our motto be "We seek God" and to know God and live in the nourishment and vitality he brings and can bring to us.

No longer shall we live in the clutches of toxic and limiting faith. Instead, we shall be determined to follow the broad and practical guides for living found in balanced Christian beliefs. What a goal for the coming year (and for the years to come)! Amen.

Epilogue

I hope your journey through the pages of this book has assisted in bringing encouragement and healing. The guiding purpose was to bring some direction in the wilderness between crisis of belief and arriving to a place of stability again. The wilderness could be a crisis of belief from a toxic family or religious system, spiritual abuse, false beliefs, growth from previous belief structures, or even boredom with your prior beliefs.

I have sought to bring pastoral care and counseling themes into the chapters that we all need, especially when going through or in recovery from crisis. In a crisis, the temptation is to throw everything overboard or to "throw the baby out with the bathwater," as the saying goes. May I, gently and respectfully, suggest that there could be a better way that provides retaining the good and claiming the healthy parts of your old experience.

Finding ourselves in a wilderness of confused belief, however, can be frightening. My hope is that this book truly provided some signposts on the journey back to faith. May the blessings of God be with you and may you come to enjoy your spiritual journey and be at peace!

References

1. I believe this description was first used by retired Episcopal Bishop John Shelby Spong.
2. Earlier versions of this chapter are from J. LeBron McBride, "Leaving an Unhealthy Church: How to Survive the Transition Trauma" *The Plain Truth*, July/August (2006): 22–25 and J. LeBron McBride, "How to Leave a Church and Survive the Wilderness," *Proclamation*, November / December (2005): 10–15 and some themes can also be found in J. LeBron McBride, *Living Faithfully with Disappointment in the Church*, NY: Routledge, 2005.
3. Unless otherwise noted, scripture verses are from *The Holy Bible, New International Version*, 1973, 1978 by the International Bible Society. Used by permission of Zondervan Bible Publishers.
4. Information about this can be found at: https://smithhouse.com/our-history/smith-house-mine-shaft/. Accessed 4/36/17.
5. *The Holy Bible,* King James Version, 1611, Psalms 40:1–3.
6. Ibid., Ps. 40:2b.
7. www.kentcrockett.com_Kent Crockett's Sermon Illustrations, Accessed 05/21/2017.
8. Used with permission of the writer.
9. *The Holy Bible,* New English Translation. Cambridge: Oxford University Press, 1961, Luke 3:15.
10. Commonly attributed to Goethe but note this webpage by the Goethe Society: http://www.goethesociety.org/pages/quote-scom.html, The Queen's Christmas Carol; An Anthology of Poems, Stories, Essays, Drawings and Music by British Authors,

Artists and Composers (author unknown). London: Daily Mail, 1905. Accessed 05/21/2017.

11. Source Unknown. https://bible.org/illustration/out-darkness. Accessed 05/21/2017

12. Johann Wolfgang von Goethe, http://www.wiseoldsayings.com/fate-quotes/. Accessed 5/10/2017.

13. Martin Luther King, Jr, "The Drum Major Instinct" (169–186) in *A Knock at Midnight: Inspiration from the Great Sermons of Reverend Martin Luther King, Jr.* ed. Clayborne Carson and Peter Holloran, 1998. NY: IPM in association with Warner Books; Copyright 1997, The Heirs to the Estate of Martin Luther King, Jr.

14. Ibid., p. 177.

15. Ibid., p. 182.

16. Watchmen Nee, Table in Wilderness: Daily Devotional Meditations from the Ministry of *Watchman Nee*, Fort Washington, PA: Christian Literature Crusade, 1969, April 19.

17. Fred Craddock, *Craddock Stories.* ed. Mike Graves and Richard F. Ward. St. Louis: Chalice Press, 2001. p. 94.

18. Eric Hoffer. *The True Believer: Thought on the Nature of Mass Movements.* 1st edition. NY: Harper and Brothers, 1951.

19. Frederick Buechner, *Wishful Thinking: A Doubter's Dictionary,* San Francisco: Harper Collins, 1988, p. 30.

20. Madeleine L'Engle. *The Mythical Bible.* http://www.30goodminutes.org/index.php/archives/23-member-archives/469-madeleine-l-engle-program-3501, First air date January 6, 1991., Copyright, 2017, Chicago Sunday Evening Club. Accessed 05/21/2017.

21. Joan Chittister *The Role of Religion in Today's Society.* http://www.30goodminutes.org/index.php/archives/23-member-archives/469-madeleine-l-engle-program-3501, First air date, November, 24, 1991. Copyright, 2017, Chicago Sunday Evening Club. Accessed 05/21/2017.

22. Original material was from a sermon I wrote for the Community Holy Week Services, at Second Ave Baptist Church, Rome, GA, April 18, 2011.

23. Robert M. Brown, *The Significance of the Church*. Philadelphia: Westminster Press, 1956, p.17.

24. Keith Miller. *The Taste of New Wine*. Waco, Texas: Word Books, 1965, p. 22.

25. Clovis Chapel. *Faces about the Cross*. New York: Abingdon-Cokesbury Press, 1941.

26. Herbert Anderson. *Mighty Rituals*. San Francisco: Jossey-Bass, 2001, p. 159.

27. The source of the proverb isn't known; It was used 1858 in *Songs and Ballads* by Samuel Lover; http://treepony.com/phrase-origins-the-darkest-hour-is-just-before-dawn/. Accessed 05/21/2013.

28. Thomas Connelan reference unknown found on *Kent Crockett's Sermon Illustrations*; http://www.kentcrockett.com/cgi-bin/illustrations/index.cgi?topic=Motivation. Accessed 05/20/2017.

29. *The Holy Bible*, New Revised Standard, Massachusetts: Hendrickson Publishers, Inc. National Council of Church in U. S. of America, 1989. Psalm 30.5b.

30. William Sloane Coffin, *The Collected Works of William Sloane Coffin: The Riverside Years, Vol 2*. Louisville: Westminster, 2008, p.29.

31. Unknown author used by William H. Willimon in sermon at Duke University Chapel May 23, 1999.

32. J. LeBron McBride, *Living Faithfully with Disappointment in the Church*. New York: Haworth, Press, 2005. P. *xiv*.

33. Paul Tillich, *The New Being*. NY: Charles Scriber's Son, 1995.

34. Marcus Borg, *Reading the Bible Again of the First Time: Taking the Bible Seriously but not Literally*. San Francisco: Harper, 2002.

35. Karen Armstrong, *"My Wish: The Charter for Compassion,"* *Ted Talk*. March, 2008 https://www.ted.com/talks/karen_arm-

strong_makes_her_ted_prize_wish_the_charter_for_compassion/transcript?language=en. Accessed 05/21/2017.

36. This chapter is derived in part from an earlier version I wrote that was published in: Copyright 2007, *Pastoral Care from the Pulpit: Meditations of Hope and Encouragement* by J. LeBron McBride. Reproduced by permission of Taylor and Francis Group, LLC, a division of Informa plc.

37. Clifford Green, *Karl Barth: Theologian of Freedom*. Minneapolis: Fortress Press, 1991, page. 16 (mentioned but no footnote given).

38. Houston Smith, *The Soul of Christianity*: Restoring the Great Tradition. San Francisco: Harper Collins, 2005, p. 47.

39. Selected from Charles Smith. *Just Plain Funny*. Pittsburgh: Rosedog Press, 2012.

40. Paul Tillich, op. cit., Chapter 18, p. 56.

41. Ibid.

42. Marcus Borg, *Reading the Bible Again for the First Time: Taking the Bible Seriously but not Literally*. San Francisco: Harper Collins, 1989, p. 254.

43. Ibid. Marcus Borg quotes from Robin Scroggs in *Paul for a New Day*. Philadelphia Fortress Press, 1977, p. 10.

44. Arthur C. Zepp, "Conscience Alone Not a Safe Guide" Chicago: The Christian Writers Company. 1903, p. 103 in *Healing for Damage Emotions Workbook: A Recovery Workbook for Healing Damaged Emotions* by David A Seamands and Beth Funk. Colorado Spring: David Cook Publications, 2004, p. 106.

45. Stephen Covey, *The Seven Habits of Highly Effective People*. NY: Fireside, 1990, p. 33 (quoted by Caleb Rosado in *Paradigm Shifts and Stages of Societal Change* below).

46. Caleb Rosado, *Paradigm Shifts and Stages of Societal Change: A Descriptive Model*, Rosado Consulting for Change in Human Systems, 1997. http://www.rosado.net/pdf/Paradigms.pdf.

47. Peter Marshall, Keeping Christmas in *The Best of Peter Marshall*. ed. Catherine Marshall. NY: Guideposts Chosen Books, 1983.

48. Author unknown. Used often on internet for example: *Sermons Central.* https://www.sermoncentral.com/sermons/all-saints-c-roger-haugen-sermon-on-god-the-father-41988. Accessed 05/21/217.

49. Robert Louis Stevenson, Quoted in: *The Wisdom of the Great* by Sam Majdi. Bloomington, IN: iUniverse, 2012, p. 351.

50. Mary Anderson, "Living by the Word: Blind Spots: Mark 10:46–52," *The Christian Century;* October, 2003, p. 21.

51. Charles Spurgeon, Spurgeon's Expository Encyclopedia. Grand Rapids: Baker Book House, Vol.8, 1984, p. 489.

52. Dale Robbins. *Complaining Only Makes Things Worse.* VL-105. http://www.victorious.org/pub/stop-complaining-105. Accessed 5/1/17. Used by permission. Copyright by Dr. Dale Robbins, 1990–2017.

53. Author unknown.

54. SL Gable, HT Reis, EA Impett, ER Asher. "What do you do when things go right? The intrapersonal and interpersonal benefits of sharing positive events." *Journal of Personality and Social Psychology*, 2004; 87; 2, pp. 228–345.

55. Viktor. E. Frankl, *Man's Search for Meaning: An Introduction to Logotherapy.* Beacon Press, 2006, p. 86. (Originally published in 1946).

56. Steve Goodier, Quote Magazine, in *Reader's Digest*, May, 1990.

57. Erma Bombeck, Me Have Cancer! *Reader's Digest* 142, April, 1993, pp. 96–98.

58. Barbara Brown Taylor, *Speaking of Sin: The Lost Language of Salvation.* Boston: Cowley Publications, 2000, p. 58.

59. Ibid., p. 58.

60. William J. Doherty, See How They Run: When Did Childhood Turn into A Rat Race? *The Family Networker*, 2003, 38, 46, 63.

61. Maggie Ross, Barking at Angels, In *Weaving: A Journal of the Christian Spiritual Life*. January/February, 2006; pp. 13–17, p. 16. Nashville: Upper Room Ministries.

62. Dante. Alighieri, *The Divine Comedy: Inferno:* Quoted in *Darkness Visible* by William Styron. Random House, 1990, p. 82.

63. http://www.ethicsdaily.com/tis-the-season-for-what-cms-5080 James L. Evans is pastor of Auburn First Baptist Church in Auburn, AL." 'Tis The Season, For What?" December 8, 2004 *Ethics Daily.* Accessed 5/21/17.

64. Ibid.

65. Dante Alighieri, *The Divine Comedy: Inferno* Quoted in *Darkness Visible* by William Styron. Random House, 1990, p. 82.

66. Barbara Brown Taylor, Expecting the Second Coming. *Christian Century,* September 21, 2004, p. 38.

67. Frederick Buechner, *Wishful Thinking: A Seeker's ABC.* San Francisco: Harper Collins, 1988, p. 79.

68. Borg. Markus. *The Heart of Christianity: Rediscovering the Life of Faith.* San Francisco: HarperCollins, 2003, p. 180.

69. Barbara Brown Taylor, *Christian Century,* September 21, 2004, p 38.

70. F. Scott Fitzgerald. The Crack-Up. *Esquire.* Three-part series February, March, and April, 1936, p. 78.

71. Martin Marty, *A Cry of Absence: Reflections for the Winter of the Heart.* San Francisco: Harper and Row, 1983, p. 1.

72. Attributed to Arthur Schopenhauer by Martin Luther King, Jr. in *A Knock at Midnight,* op. cit. p. 70. However, I have never been able to find the original source.

73. Peter Marshall, "Keeping Christmas" in *The Best of Peter Marshall.* ed. by Catherine Marshall. NY: Guideposts Chosen Books, 1983, p. 106

74. Fred Craddock, op. cit., p. 140

About the Author

Dr. J. LeBron McBride has twenty years of experience as an ordained minister and almost thirty as a licensed family therapist. The last church he pastored was First Christian Church (Disciples of Christ) of Rome, Georgia, where he was senior minister for twelve years. He worked for many years as a minister while at another position.

Currently, he is the Director of Behavioral Medicine, Director of the Medical Student Clerkship, and a faculty member with the Floyd Medical Center Family Medicine Residency Program. He is the author of over a hundred published items, including five books. (In addition to this book are the following: *Spiritual Crisis: Surviving Trauma to the Soul, Family Behavioral Issues in Health and Illness, Living Faithfully with Disappointment in the Church*, and *Pastoral Care from the Pulpit*, all with Taylor & Francis–Routledge Press.)

He holds clinical appointments with several medical schools including Nova University, the Medical College of Georgia, and Mercer University. He obtained his PhD in marriage and family therapy from Florida State University, a master's degree in public health from Loma Linda University, and graduated with high honors with a master's of divinity degree from Andrews University. A licensed family therapist, Dr. McBride is a fellow and an approved supervisor with the American Association of Marriage and Family Therapists and is a credential pastoral counselor and fellow in the American Association of Pastoral Counselors.

He and his wife, Deborah, a family nurse practitioner, have two adult children and live on a farm outside of Rome. Dr. McBride writes from the perspective of having spent countless hours listening to persons in therapy and in pastoral care situations. He seeks to deal with the hard realities of life with a positive approach that brings hope and comfort to persons in difficulty.

CPSIA information can be obtained
at www.ICGtesting.com
Printed in the USA
BVHW08s1713130618
518945BV00005B/255/P